PUTTING CHILDREN FIRST

A Guide for Parents Breaking Up

This book describes a child-centred approach for separated and divorcing parents who want to minimize the damage done to children during and after the break-up. It offers essential information and advice on renegotiating the practical and emotional aspects of the parent–child relationship.

Hanna McDonough and Christina Bartha are leading clinicians in their field and use their extensive experience in counselling families to provide a step-by-step guide to the emotional work parents must do to make their divorce manageable for themselves and their children. They also highlight the relevant research findings concerning the effects of divorce on families. Recent studies show that it is not only the presence of conflict that determines the adjustment of children to their parents' divorce, but the way in which parents involve their children in their conflict with each other.

HANNA MCDONOUGH, MSW, CSW, is the Clinical Consultant to the 'For Kids' Sake' Program at the Clarke Division in the Centre for Addiction and Mental Health and Lecturer in the Department of Psychiatry at the University of Toronto.

CHRISTINA BARTHA, MSW, CSW, is the Administrative Director and clinical social worker in the Mood and Anxiety Disorders Program at the Clarke Division in the Centre for Addiction and Mental Health.

PUTTING CHILDREN FIRST

A Guide for Parents Breaking Up

Hanna McDonough and Christina Bartha

UNIVERSITY OF TORONTO PRESS
Toronto Buffalo London
© University of Toronto Press Incorporated 1999

© University of Toronto Press Incorporated 1999
Toronto Buffalo London
Printed in Canada

ISBN 0-8020-4217-1 (cloth)
ISBN 0-8020-8064-2 (paper)

Printed on acid-free paper

Canadian Cataloguing in Publication Data

McDonough, Hanna
    Putting children first : a guide for parents breaking up

    Includes bibliographical references and index.
    ISBN 0-8020-4217-1 (bound)   ISBN 0-8020-8064-2 (pbk.)

    1. Divorce – Psychological aspects. 2. Separation (Psychology).
    3. Marital conflict. 4. Conflict management. 5. Children of divorced
    parents – Psychology. I. Bartha, Christina. II. Title.

    HQ814.M32 1999   306.89   C99-930204-3

University of Toronto Press acknowledges the financial assistance of the
Canada Council for the Arts and the Ontario Arts Council to its publishing
program.

Contents

Introduction

A DIVORCED PARENT'S REGRET

I survived a long and bloody custody dispute. It wiped out five years of my life and cost me more than $50,000.00. And we did not even make it to trial!

The dispute created scars that will never go away. Our son is scarred, we are scarred, and together we limp toward some broken future, emotionally, financially, and spiritually exhausted.

In the legal system, you focus on problems instead of solutions. You watch what is going on in your ex's home instead of your own. Your children, loving both of you, are caught in the middle. Because going to court promises a 'win,' we get hooked. After a bad break-up you want to 'win,' you want revenge. So we litigated and litigated, and it was a nightmare.

I wish I had never gone to court. I wish I had calmed down. My ex is not a terrible man or a terrible father, but for six years that's how I saw him, and fought him ... tooth and nail.

And why? Because I was in pain. Did the fighting help? No. I just had to accept I could not change what was going on at his father's. When I did, I stopped fighting.

If you only realized that when you first separate you are temporarily insane, you would not fight and your kids would be spared.

A DIVORCED PARENT'S RELIEF

It was the hardest thing I have ever done, but I did it, and we are now okay ... all of us. Four years ago, I left my husband and took my two children. We fought and quarrelled, and finally managed a co-operative divorce.

Recently we have started co-parenting and I feel great about it. It was the hardest thing ever. We were not good candidates for co-operative parenting because we weren't even speaking. When my husband had an affair, I wanted to kill, *not co-operate*. He deserved to lose his children for what he did to me. I was fit to be tied.

The children, 10 and 7, were depressed when we split. They blamed me because they were very close to Jim. It bothered me that they took his side. We got lawyers, settled the divorce. Jim did not want to fight: I got custody, he got every second weekend. I resented every minute he got.

While I was angry all over the place, I noticed how the kids treated me after their time with their father. They were tender with me. I wondered about it. One day the older one thanked me for letting them see their father. He said he knew how hard it was for me. I could not believe his maturity. I thought, if my kid could be so mature, what about me?

I went for counselling to explore my marriage, and why it broke down, and I cried. I really loved Jim and we had drifted apart. In all those years I was too afraid to lose him to discuss our relationship. He had often wanted to talk about it but I always shut him down.

I have now put aside my anger and started talking to Jim. We now plan for the kids together. The kids split their weeks between us and we live two streets apart. Jim is a good person ... I wish we were still together. The kids are so happy he is their father. They look at me with love in their eyes. I feel their gratitude. I'm so glad I didn't wreck it for them. But it was close!

BE AWARE AND BEWARE

In North America, 40 to 50 per cent of marriages end in divorce.

Most couples separate 'amicably' or in 'a disengaged way,' and conflicts lessen in two to three years. Children in these divorces suffer only temporary adjustment problems.

About 25 per cent of divorces remain intensely conflicted (Maccoby & Mnookin, 1992). A smaller number of couples (10 per cent) litigate. They go to court but do not settle. These are the high-conflict divorces – the 'divorces from hell' (Dennis, 1996). The fighting continues and becomes central to the family's life. Children in these divorces suffer real damage. Research shows that it is not the divorce but the *fighting*, and the ways parents use their children in that fighting, that harms children (Johnston et al., 1987; Wallerstein & Kelly, 1980; Hetherington et al., 1982; Kelly, 1993).

A family disruption results in enormous loss, which requires grieving. Fighting is a stage in that process. Some parents get stuck there and keep fighting. The tragedy is that when you fight, you do not tend to your children. The fighting absorbs you and makes you neglect or distort your children's needs. When you are fighting, you do not notice how caught up you are in it. You think it is the other parent's fault. You do not notice how you are hurting your children. Although fighting is a very poor way of managing family problems, it is sanctioned by the legal system.

In this book we focus on *parental conflict* because it is common right after the separation, and if you do not manage it carefully it can lead to a child's worst nightmare: very limited care by both parents, conflicted access with the child caught in the middle, and, if that continues, the possible loss of a parent.

Conflict is not the only factor that determines a child's adjustment after divorce. The well-being of the parent with whom the child lives, and the quality of the child's relationships with both parents are as important. The tightened finances of families after divorce, as well as restricted time with a parent take their toll on children.

That being said, we focus on conflict because it is one of the most important variables determining a child's post-divorce adjustment (Amato & Keith, 1991), and because *conflict is something over which you have total control.*

This book will help you do the emotional work you need to do to avoid fighting and to parent successfully after divorce. The tense and hostile atmosphere after divorce can lead to disputes. To break up without fighting, you have to have your wits about you. Just as it only takes *one* of you to start a fight, it often takes only *one* of you to prevent or stop that fight.

Informed as it is by current research and best practice, this book makes you both AWARE and BEWARE. We offer you the most relevant research, theory, and practice so that you will know exactly what to do to get out of the tough situation you find yourself in right after separating. Once you understand separation and conflict, and their effect on your kids, you will be able to manage your situation with care. We deal with the issues that arise in all divorces: grieving, moving on in your life, the parenting plan, residential arrangements and decision-making, problems of shared time, and going to court. We offer tips on how to manage yourself, your partner, and your children. We talk about separations with disturbing allegations, about how to reintroduce absent parents to children, and about parental alienation syndrome and supervised access.

This book will help you avoid conflict, and manage conflict if you are in it. And if you must go to court, it will help you do 'damage control.' In managing divorce, it is always best to avoid conflict; and if conflict is unavoidable it is important to end it as quickly as possible. And finally, if protecting your children means there is no alternative to court, it is important for you to be court-smart.

Most of all, this book is your *survival kit*. It gives you complete and easy-to-read directions on how to do the emotional work you need to do in order for you and your children to survive your separation in good shape. When it is all said and done, and the crisis is over, what will matter is whether you did the right thing. If you do what this book tells you to, you will have done the right thing and your children will thank you for it.

The Reason for This Book

This book comes from our clinical and research experience with divorcing families. We have been inspired by those parents who co-operate. They have taught us how, for the sake of their children, parents can find creative ways to put aside their differences. We have also been alarmed by the number of 'divorces from hell' (Dennis, 1996). For these situations, we have developed helpful strategies in a program called 'For Kids' Sake' (McDonough et al., 1994; see appendix).

The good news is that when parents stop blaming each other and focus on their children, the fighting stops and the kids become unburdened. The bad news is that family disruption is painful and requires all of a parent's maturity, good will, and self-discipline to ensure that it does not get out of hand and damage the children.

The Politics of Custody Disputes

Separation is not just a family affair – it also involves the judiciary and the state. When you cannot arrive at plans for your children, the judiciary steps in to make those plans for you. As a result, many parents have formed groups through which to express their discontent with the courts and with the decisions they make. These groups work to increase public awareness about issues in custody and access planning. There are fathers' rights groups, mother's rights groups, and groups for abused partners and abused children.

We understand the points of view of these diverse groups and have worked with them over the years. We believe that each group has a hold of *part* of the truth in the larger picture of post-divorce social and family dilemmas. Sadly, these various groups have at times become as polarized as the parents in high-conflict divorces. Our focus in this book is on the element that unifies all these groups: the child's interests and the child's point of view.

The Child's Point of View

We take the child's point of view, and make no excuse for it. In divorce, it is the child's development, not that of the parents, that is at risk. A child is vulnerable, a work in progress, and needs both of you, regardless of the crises you face. When you divorce, you hope for better times, but your children cannot put their lives on hold. For them, *now* is what counts.

In the management of divorce, our children are our main responsibility. And because children absolutely need unconflicted closeness to their parents, we must try to provide it. As parents we may feel responsible for many things in our lives: our relationships, our families, our work, our activities, our friendships, our children. But in fact, we are only *really* responsible for our children, because their growth depends on us (and on those to whom we delegate that responsibility). Our other undertakings do not depend only on us for their well-being; our children *do*. No one else will take care of them like we do. How they turn out reflects our care.

There is a two-way bond between parents and children, a back-and-forth, a check-and-balance. As parents, we act as a mirror: we try to provide our children with an accurate appreciation of who they are and what they need; and at the same time, we see some of ourselves reflected in them. This makes us aware of our strengths and of where we need to grow. To be a parent is to be always nudged beyond our limitations. In this light, to be a parent undergoing a separation is to be profoundly nudged beyond our limitations.

We make no excuses for our challenging approach. We have learned that when families are stuck, they need a strong approach. One of our mothers, in a bitter dispute with a once-loved spouse, could not see what part she was playing in the fighting. 'But you're hurting your son as much as his father is.' She stopped in her tracks, thought about it, and agreed. Later she told us she wished we had confronted her sooner.

An Alternative to Conflict

We offer insight, reflection, honesty, and self-management as alternatives to conflict. When one of you pulls out of the power struggle, it stops. As one mother put it, 'It's like a tug of war – if you let the rope go, it's over.'

Our Philosophy of Separating

Although divorced, you are still a family – a separated family, but a family nonetheless. Taking this attitude helps. Unless a child is in danger from the other parent's behaviour, you must include each other fully. It takes maturity to include rather than exclude, and your struggle to be mature results in a richer life for your kids. Remember that you are divorcing each other, not your children. Staying connected encourages your children's ties to you, your extended family, and relatives and friends on both sides. These connections often spark your children's interests: 'I learned fishing from my father's uncle ...'

After separation, the question is not whether to keep your children closely connected to both of you, but how.

Housekeeping

We have altered our case examples to protect confidentiality. To avoid the win/lose tone of legal jargon, we have replaced 'custodial' and 'access' with 'residential' and 'nonresidential.' Sometimes in discussing imposed parental plans, we have used the shorter term 'access parent'; but this is in no way to diminish that parent's role. To keep it simple, and because it reflects how things are, we usually refer to mothers as residential parents and fathers as nonresidential or access parents. Similarly, we refer to the child sometimes as 'he,' other times as 'she.' Finally, we use the terms 'separation' and 'divorce' interchangeably. We consider it unimportant to family dynamics whether you were married, or lived common-law, or had a shorter term relationship. The dynamics we discuss apply to parents regardless of their official status.

ACKNOWLEDGMENTS

We thank our families from the Family Court Clinic, the 'For Kids' Sake' program, and the Separated Parents' Forums. We particularly thank our volunteer parents, especially Judy and Lee. We are greatly indebted to Helen Scott Goudge, MSW, CSW, for her thoughtful clinical discussions and for writing the chapter on the parenting plan. We thank Dr Eric Hood for the meticulous editing of the first part, and Dr Helen Radovanovic for her suggestions. We cannot thank Kelly Marcil, our secretary, enough for her generous and expert support. We are also indebted to Joan Santiago and Ilse Mozga from the Clarke Library.

We have borrowed heavily from the knowledge and research of Janet Johnston, Judith Wallerstein, Joan Kelly, and Mavis Hetherington. They have contributed much to our understanding of divorce and high conflict and their effect on families.

On a more personal note, many thanks to Christopher and David for their love and encouragement.

Part I

Preventing Conflict

1. Three Different Kinds of Divorce

There are three kinds of divorces, with very different effects on children (Maccoby & Mnookin, 1992).

THE AMICABLE DIVORCE

The easiest for children is the 'amicable divorce,' where you, as parents, talk to each other freely about your children, with little hostility. Your children enjoy a full relationship with both of you. Because you do not want to exclude each other, your children feel they are allowed to speak to you about the time they spend with the other. When the child has a problem with one of you, she can discuss it with the other, and it gets resolved. Together, you adjust the parenting plan to your child's changing needs.

Children in amicable divorces are close to both their parents at the same time. For instance, both parents come to the school play. At one parent's home, the child feels comfortable phoning the other parent; or the child may use dad's help to make a Mother's Day card. This degree of comfort allows children to develop a stronger sense of themselves. Children in amicable divorces still feel they belong to a larger family – or more exactly, two families.

On being asked about her favourite memories, a 16-year-old in an amicable divorce said, 'My sixteenth birthday was my favourite because my parents bought me a stereo. Whenever I look at the stereo, I think, "Wow ... my parents loved me enough to put aside their differences for me." That felt like real love.'

THE DISENGAGED DIVORCE

A disengaged divorce also allows children good connection to both parents, who manage their hostility by avoiding contact with each other. The couple are 'disengaged' from each other, but not from their children. Planning for the children often occurs through the child (when old enough) or a third party. Children are close to their parents and are spared conflict, and this allows them to grow and develop.

Research shows that parents of younger children tend to interact more, because their children require it. When children are old enough to take part in communicating, parents often become more disengaged from each other (Maccoby & Mnookin, 1992). Most co-operative divorces use the disengaged style.

Twelve-year-old Judy's parents were 'disengaged.' When asked how she felt about arranging the visits, Judy replied, 'It was hard when I was younger, but now it's second nature and doesn't bother me at all.' She thought having to be a 'go-between' a small price to pay for good relations.

As parents in a disengaged divorce, you 'let sleeping dogs lie.' Because you fought whenever you talked, you learned to back off. This is often a very good thing to do. In a program for high-conflict divorces at Toronto's Clarke Division, 'For Kids' Sake' (see page 178), our goal with highly conflicted families is to help them become disengaged. When they become disengaged, we call it success.

Children from disengaged divorces are not damaged because they are protected from any fighting (Maccoby and Mnookin, 1992). This same research shows that over time, some disengaged couples become co-operative and amicable.

THE HIGH-CONFLICT DIVORCE

Parents in highly conflicted divorces are still fighting three or more years after separation. These relationships involve deep mistrust, poor communication, mutual denigration, allegations, and sometimes abuse. Parents in conflicted divorces take polarized positions: they view themselves as all good and the other parent as all bad. Each parent sees the other as the entire problem.

Children caught in these conflicts live in war zones and often develop signs of distress such as stomachaches and temper tantrums (Johnston et al., 1987). Their symptoms are similar to those of children who have suffered trauma. If the fighting continues, they develop emotional, behavioural, and social problems such as aggression, oppositional behaviour, difficulties in school, and conduct disorder (Guidubaldi & Perry, 1985; Hetherington, et al. 1982; and see Chapter 10). It is the feeling of being caught between their parents that creates the greatest stress for children (Buchanan et al., 1991; Johnston et al., 1989).

When you create this kind of hostile atmosphere, you are really harming your children. You harm them when you *expose* them to your conflict and also when you *use* them in your conflict. You *must* stop fighting; and if you can't, your contact with them will have to be restricted in order to protect them. Transfers from one parent to the other will have to be supervised so as not to expose them to fighting. If the fighting continues, one parent's contact will have to be restricted, and the children may eventually lose a parent. To allow this to happen is a tragic waste.

A 19-year-old child of a high-conflict divorce describes her experience: 'I feel torn between my parents all day long. If I agree with one, I offend the other. If I'm mad at my mother, I don't talk about it' 'cause my dad gets off on it. I don't even tell them about my school plays any more because I can't deal with the fight about who comes, who sits where, and with whom. Many times I have felt suicidal, and desperately alone. I really can't talk to either one. Anything I say becomes grist for their mill. I don't exist for them.

'And you know something funny? Although they accuse each other of being terrible parents, I think, outside of their fighting, they are both fine. Because of the fighting, I am destroyed by both.'

WHAT KIND OF A DIVORCE ARE YOU CREATING?

This is the most important question you have to ask yourself.

Be glad if you are creating *an amicable divorce*. It will not hurt your children as long as you attend to them. When they reach 6 or 7 years of age, and again when they are teenagers, you will need to discuss with them the reasons for your divorce. This information, and your openness about it, will help your children develop a more positive picture of marriage.

The 16-year-old mentioned earlier told us she had 'a cynical view of marriage' and did not trust long-term relationships. She was not even hoping for one. She said that in this she was different from her friends in intact families: 'They believe in love. I don't. I often find myself thinking they are being way too gullible. I know I'm cynical, but I can't help it.'

If you are creating a *disengaged divorce*, be happy. This arrangement allows your children to have a good relationship with both of you. You have shown maturity in containing your hostility. Maybe later, when you are less angry and hurt, you may be able to develop a more amicable divorce. Or maybe not – some divorces do not become amicable, no matter how hard the parents try. If this is your situation, instead of trying to improve your relationship with the other parent, put your energy into communicating with your child. Encourage her to tell you what it is like for her to have you two not speaking to each other, or to have to act as a go-between.

Nine-year-old Geoff had to call his father whenever his mother was late. As manager of a restaurant, she could not always leave work at the arranged times. He understood this, but he still hated calling his dad. His dad was often annoyed, and Geoff was sensitive to it. His mother decided to ask Geoff how he felt having to call his father when she was late.

When she brought up the topic, at first Geoff was defensive. He thought she was going to tell him off. But she kept at it, and finally he understood that she really wanted to know how he felt. He said he hated her being late, because he then had to call his dad, who got annoyed. He complained about being 'in the middle.' His mother listened. She placed her arm around his shoulders and said, 'I can see how hard this is for you. It puts extra demands on you, and you feel responsible. You aren't responsible, we are, and I'm sorry we don't manage a better way.' She then invited him to tell her whenever he was upset.

Some parents feel bad about not being able to talk amicably to their partners. Sometimes you just have to cut your losses. Geoff's mother was angry that she and her spouse were not managing better. But at the same time, she needed to make allowances. Their marriage had been bitter and they were managing their divorce as best they could. She needed to remember that this divorce was good enough and not hurting Geoff. It frustrated him, but as long as he could express it, he was fine.

In amicable and disengaged divorces, children have good relationships with both parents. The details of the parenting plan are less important than the achievement of co-operation and shared parenting. Any number of parenting arrangements are possible: shared parenting, co-parenting, joint custody, dual home, split time, alternate weekends, or whatever. As long as children younger than three get more time with one parent, and as long as the parents co-operate, children can usually manage any plan.

In parenting plans, the goal is to provide each child with as much *living* time with each parent as possible. Note that we say 'living' as opposed to 'visiting.' Children in these divorces feel they have three families, not that they have one family and are 'visiting' the other family. In other words, the children have predictable routine time with each parent. Each family works this out in its own way and most try to separate siblings to allow each child some time alone with each parent.

The success of these plans lies in the way your love for your children translates into an unbroken life for them.

If you think your relationship with your partner is – or is evolving into – a *high-conflict divorce*, take action immediately. Learn about how conflict affects your child. Lay down your arms. Do not assume that the other parent is the problem. If you cannot reduce the conflict, go for counselling immediately. Most chronic conflicts need skilled intervention.

If you feel you must take the other parent to court to protect your child's safety, be sure the child really is in danger and that your fears have a basis in reality. These situations can be very confusing. Obtain a clinical assessment to validate your concerns, and then resolve the problem, taking great care not to escalate it (see Chapter 12).

- Be clear about which kind of divorce you are creating, and its effect on your children.
- If you are in an amicable divorce, don't let it become disengaged.
- If you are in a disengaged divorce, don't let it escalate into a high-conflict one. Try to develop amicable behaviours.
- If you are in a high-conflict divorce, get help immediately.
- If you have serious child protection concerns, contact a child welfare agency and then obtain a clinical assessment.

2. The Stresses of Divorce and the Loss of Love

WHY IS DIVORCE SO STRESSFUL?

Divorce is highly stressful because it is about loss. Loss of what is most near and dear to you: your intimate relationship and full-time parenting. In the next two chapters we will deal with each of these losses in turn.

But for now, let us look at why divorce is so stressful. Divorce is so stressful because it affects every part of your life. Divorce is not a simple event like selling your home. It is a multifaceted process that takes years to complete. It is a complex social, familial, and personal experience. Ending an intimate relationship is traumatic in itself; ending your family, as you now know it, is also traumatic. When you are divorcing with children, you are taking a huge double-hit.

Because divorce is more common now than it was twenty years ago, some people downplay its impact: 'Oh, it's just an adjustment, you'll get over it soon.' People who minimize the stress involved in divorce are doing you a disservice. Divorce is a huge, painful adjustment, and those who say otherwise don't appreciate the emotional work involved.

David came for counselling because his 4-year-old daughter Sacha would not sleep by herself since her parents separated. He knew she was upset, and he was frantic to get her to talk about her sadness. When asked about his own adjustment to the separation, he said he was fine, and 'soldiering through.' He had not altered his hectic pace or taken time to deal with his feelings. In fact, he had not even told his friends at work about it. When he was coached to help Sacha discuss the day her mother moved out of the family home, he became tearful. Through his daughter's sadness, his own grief surfaced. He and his daughter cried together about that very sad day.

The Divorces within a Divorce

Divorce is a many-layered process, a little like peeling the proverbial onion: When you take off one layer, there is always another underneath. When couples divorce, many relationships come to an end: lover, friend, companion, and co-parent. To part ways, parents must divorce legally, financially and socially (Bohannan, 1970). These various divorces cannot be achieved all at once, and some will take many years. Divorce also involves realigning your relationships with friends and with extended family on both sides.

Many couples end their sexual relationship while they are still married. The parental divorce begins when one of you moves out of the home and you begin to change your spousal relationship into a business one. Although the two of you stop parenting together in the same house, both of you are parents for life. The 'emotional' or 'spousal' divorce takes the longest to achieve. Because your identity became mixed up with that of your spouse, it can take years for the two of you to 'uncouple.' Uncoupling involves each of you becoming separate and independent. Uncoupling usually ends the fighting.

For those of you who were not independent going into the marriage, becoming separate will be a new achievement. Others of you will have had a clear and developed sense of yourselves, which you now have to reclaim. You know you are emotionally divorced when you no longer react emotionally to your ex-spouse. An emotional divorce paves the way for a 'good' divorce (see Chapter 4) and a good parenting plan.

Divorce as a Crazy Time

Divorcing couples say they feel like they are going through an emotional wringer. As Bohannan (1970) points out, each of the divorces within your divorce brings out a different emotion. The spousal divorce leaves you angry and hurt. The legal divorce bewilders and confuses.

Jim complained, 'You feel like you're in one of those ancient, high mazes – you can't see what's going on or where it all leads. You're in your lawyer's hands, and you just hope he knows what he's doing – otherwise you're a goner!'

The negotiations involved in the financial divorce can put you on edge and make you worry about being cheated. The parental divorce brings out your guilt about the children, and for some of you a power struggle over time and ownership. In the social divorce, you feel sad and angry if you have to divide up your friends and relations. And lastly, for some of you being alone again is a terrible experience. Given all these reactions, is it any wonder that divorce is a high-stress event?

The Stress Rating for Divorce

Stress has been a topic of research for years. We want to understand what causes stress, why we are prone to it, and how to protect ourselves from it. In 1967, two researchers in Washington, Holmes and Rahe, devised a scale of stressful events, which they called the Social Readjustment Rating Scale. This original scale was updated in 1997 by Miller and Rahe. We include it here. (See pages 12–14.)

As you can see, divorce ranks very high as a life stressor (96 points). It ranks very closely to 'death of a spouse' (119 points) or close family number. To appreciate how stressful divorce is, notice that being laid off from work rates only 68 points, which most people would consider quite traumatic.

What Does Stress Put You at Risk For?

According to Holmes and Rahe, any change you make in your life causes stress because of the energy you have to expend to adjust to it.

Social Readjustment Rating Scale (1997)

Life change event	Points	My score
Home and family:		
Major change in living conditions	42	_____
Change in residence:		
move within the same town or city	25	_____
move to a different town, city, or state	47	_____
Change in family get-togethers	25	_____
Major change in health or behaviour of family members	55	_____
Marriage	50	_____
Pregnancy	67	_____
Miscarriage or abortion	65	_____
Gain of a new family member:		
birth of a child	66	_____
adoption of a child	65	_____
a relative moving in with you	59	_____
Spouse beginning or ending work	46	_____
Child leaving home:		
to attend college	41	_____
due to marriage	41	_____
for other reasons	45	_____
Change in arguments with spouse	50	_____
In-law problems	38	_____
Change in the marital status of your parents:		
divorce	59	_____
remarriage	50	_____
Separation from spouse:		
due to work	53	_____
due to marital problems	76	_____
Divorce	96	_____
Birth of a grandchild	43	_____
Death of a spouse	119	_____
Death of other family member:		
child	123	_____
brother or sister	102	_____
parent	100	_____

Social Readjustment Rating Scale (1997) (*Continued*)

Life change event	Points	My score
Health:		
An injury or illness which:		
kept you in bed a week or more, or sent you to the hospital	74	_____
was less serious than above	44	_____
Major dental work	26	_____
Major change in eating habits	27	_____
Major change in sleeping habits	26	_____
Major change in your usual and/or amount of recreation	28	_____
Work:		
Change to a new type of work	51	_____
Change in your work hours or conditions	35	_____
Change in your responsibilities at work:		
more responsibilities	29	_____
fewer responsibilities	21	_____
promotion	31	_____
demotion	42	_____
transfer	32	_____
Troubles at work:		
with your boss	29	_____
with coworkers	35	_____
with persons under your supervision	35	_____
other work troubles	28	_____
Major business adjustment	60	_____
Retirement	52	_____
Loss of job:		
laid off from work	68	_____
fired from work	79	_____
Correspondence course to help you in your work	18	_____
Personal and social:		
Change in personal habits	26	_____
Beginning or ending school or college	38	_____
Change of school or college	35	_____

Social Readjustment Rating Scale (1997) (*Concluded*)

Life change event	Points	My score
Personal and social: (*Continued*)		
Change in political beliefs	24	_____
Change in religious beliefs	29	_____
Change in social activities	27	_____
Vacation	24	_____
New, close, personal relationship	37	_____
Engagement to marry	45	_____
Girlfriend or boyfriend problems	39	_____
Sexual difficulties	44	_____
'Falling out' of a close personal relationship	47	_____
An accident	48	_____
Minor violation of the law	20	_____
Being held in jail	75	_____
Death of a close friend	70	_____
Major decision regarding your immediate future	51	_____
Major personal achievement	36	_____
Financial:		
Major change in finances:		
increased income	38	_____
decreased income	60	_____
investment and/or credit difficulties	56	_____
Loss of damage of personal property	43	_____
Moderate purchase	20	_____
Major purchase	37	_____
Foreclosure on a mortgage or loan	58	_____
	Total	_____

M. Miller & H. Rahe, 1997, Social Readjustment Rating Scale

Because we are creatures of habit, any change for good or bad causes stress. The higher the value attributed to an item on the scale, the greater the stress associated with that particular event.

The most recent research found that women report greater levels of stress than men when asked about the same life events. While this may mean that women are more reactive to stress, it may also mean that men tend to under-report their stress.

Some dismiss the importance of stress, saying, 'Well, stress is part of everyday life. Who is not under stress?' But stress is not just an emotional or psychological matter – it is a *health* issue. Stress attacks your immune system, and too much stress makes you susceptible to disease. Holmes and Rahe discovered that after a certain number of stressors, we became ill. In the area of divorce, their findings were very interesting. They found that in the year following divorce, couples have an illness rate twelve times higher than that for married couples. Clearly, divorce is a high-stress event for adults and children.

How to Test Your Risk for Illness Due to Stress

So let's get back to the scale. To get your score, check off the events you have experienced in the past six months in the 'My Score' column and add them up for a total score.

A score below 125 puts you at low risk for becoming ill. If you score between 125 and 199 points, the risk is moderate. If your score is between 200 and 299, the risk is elevated. A score of 300 points and over puts you at high risk of becoming ill.

Your divorce, just by itself, is 96 points. Now add to this all the other events that divorce brings with it: changes in your living conditions, 42 points, decreases in your income, 60 points. A major decision about the future is worth 51 points, while concern about the health or behaviour of your children is worth 55 points. So a typical divorce can be around 304 points. This is clearly in the high-risk range.

Why Do We Discuss the Stress Scale Here?

We are showing you the scale because we want you to realize how much stress you are under. Many parents minimize their stress. They think, 'Oh I should be managing this better. Why is this taking so long? Why is this so hard? Am I doing something wrong?' But there it is, in black and white: divorce is extremely high among life stressors.

Okay, I Am Stressed, What Do I Do?

The first thing is to *remember* that you are under extreme stress. When you remember you are under stress, you make allowances for yourself, and support yourself so that you will not harm yourself, your children, or your situation. You are careful.

The second thing is to remember how you react to stress and to anticipate your own behaviours. Then handle them carefully.

Jack knew that when he was stressed, he drank and started fights. So knowing this, he established some creative strategies for himself. He signed up for boxing at the local gym, and he made arrangements to go out with his closest buddy. He asked his friend to help him set limits on his drinking.

The third thing is to learn how to *destress* yourself. Just as it is important to know what *stresses* you, it is important to know what *destresses* you. Some people relax through hobbies or sports; others listen to music or attend arts and entertainment functions. Some need to cry or scream, some need to talk to friends. Still others seek out special forms of relaxation – massage, meditation, physical exercise, and so on.

Claire developed symptoms of anxiety after her separation. Medication helped, but she felt agitated and unfocused. She used relaxation, meditation, and massage. She also used techniques of visualization: she imagined herself and her ex resolving things in a warm and peaceful manner. These activities helped calm and soothe her. She explained that she was giving herself the message that although her spouse no longer loved her, she would nonetheless continue to love herself (as well as her children).

Claire is wise: caring for yourself, especially when significant others don't, is a sure way to shorten the time it takes to grieve. *Self-love kick-starts your grieving.* The one thing you don't want to do when you are stressed is fight. When stressed, we make 'mountains out of molehills.'

THE LOSS OF LOVE

What Does Love Mean to Me?

In our multicultural society, we marry or get into relationships for many different reasons. We marry for convenience or for the wish for children. Sometimes parents arrange marriages for dynastic, religious, or financial reasons. Some of us marry for secondary gains such as material security or immigrant status. An unplanned pregnancy can result in marriage. Or perhaps we just fall madly in love.

No matter what the reason, most couples get together hoping for love that lasts forever. 'Till death do us part' is a saying with centuries of hope behind it. We hope to have loving kindness. On the unconscious level we also secretly hope that this love will make up for all we have suffered; that it will heal every hurt of our childhood; that we will find the perfect, loving (parent?) partner. When we mate, we expect our partners to make us happy forever. This is in the invisible small print of the marriage contract.

When this does not work out, we get very upset. The distress is so hard to bear that we assign blame: we blame ourselves, our partners and our fate. 'Why me? What is wrong with me? Why couldn't I be loved? Why couldn't I *love*?'

The Intimacy, Separation, and Conflict diagram (McDonough & Hood, 1997; see next page) shows the two roads that couples in love can take. One road leads to more closeness, and the other road leads to falling out of love. Where and how these two roads fork, and which you end up taking, depends on how you deal with two things: conflict and disappointment. Couples who stay close, talk and share; those who don't, withdraw or fight. We will explain.

'Falling in love' is the springtime of a relationship. It is the way most Western couples begin a longer-term relationship. When you are in love, good will comes easily; you understand each other automatically. There seems to be no work in it. Everything about the other person is wonderful and you happily accommodate to each

INTIMACY, SEPARATION, AND CONFLICT

COUPLE IN LOVE

↓

Task: to create intimacy

↓

Successful Road ←| Problem: handling conflict and disappointment |→ Unsuccessful Road

↓ (Successful Road)

Able to tell each other what you think and feel Can talk about your differences and disappointments

↓

'More in love'

↓

CO-OPERATIVE MARRIAGE

↓ (Unsuccessful Road)

Blame/ Attack and withdraw Unable to talk about your differences and disappointments

↓

'Out of love'

↓

CONFLICTED MARRIAGE

SEPARATION

Normal Grief Reaction • can go through grieving: denial, anger, protest, disintegration, reintegration • takes 1–3 years • co-operation	**Abnormal Grief Reaction** • cannot grieve: stuck in anger phase • intolerance of sorrow, failure • reactivation of childhood trauma • fighting

↓

Amicable or Disengaged Divorces • civil behaviour • businesslike communication • child orientation	**High-Conflict Divorce** • blame, defensiveness • alienation • inability to focus on children's needs • litigation

H. McDonough, E. Hood, MD, Family Court Clinic, 1996

other. You feel blessed to have found in each other a feeling of 'home.' All you want is to be together.

With time, as you become less accommodating, you notice some less than perfect things about each other. You can handle this, but then slowly you notice more and more imperfections. You get disillusioned and disappointed, and you fall out of love. Thus, 'Was I wrong about Judy? Is she not the person I thought she was?' Judy may not be the person you thought she was, but Judy is probably how she has always been. You only knew one side of her; now she is showing you her other side. You figure you don't understand her as well as you thought you did, and you are probably right.

It is at this point that commitment is required. The understanding that was automatic at the start now has to be earned through hard work. You have to start *telling* each other your reactions, wishes, difficulties, hopes and fears. And you have to *listen*. Then you can slowly start discussing your disappointments and disagreements with each other.

Emily and Joe were crazy about each other and moved in together after dating for six weeks. Emily had never felt as close to anyone as she did to Joe. He had a way of making her feel cared about. Joe knew Emily was the one for him. His former girlfriends now seemed so dependent and undeveloped compared to Emily. After six months, Emily found Joe's love suffocating: he would not let her out of his sight. Joe, on the other hand, was surprised at the moodiness and coldness in Emily.

'Being in love' comes from how you and your partner tell each other what you are thinking and what you are feeling. This makes you feel close, and understood. This is intimacy, and it comes from staying open with each other. When you can do this, you stay close. When you cannot, you drift apart or start fighting.

You usually have no trouble communicating your *good* feelings – it is the *negative* ones that get you into trouble. Whether, as a couple, you fall more 'in love' or more 'out of love' depends specifically on how well you negotiate your conflicts and disappointments. If you can learn to discuss your differences and disappointments, you will stay in love. If you don't, and if instead you blame and withdraw, you will fall out of love.

Silence and blame lead to misunderstanding:
duo-logue leads to understanding.

So What to Do When the Going Gets Tough?

'Becoming aware' is a helpful concept to think about here. Simply put, it refers to your ability to notice and change negative patterns in your behaviour. You change them by taking control of your behaviour, deciding how you will act, and then acting the way you would like to. This is acting with self-awareness, as opposed to acting without thinking.

George felt like yelling whenever Annie overspent the budget. One day he decided he did not want to be a 'yeller.' He wanted to be rational and in control. So the next time Annie overspent, he didn't yell even though he felt like it. He talked calmly and politely. The pleasant surprise on Annie's face reflected his own.

Another Useful Concept: 'Opposites Attract'

What used to attract Emily and Joe to each other now repelled them. Joe's love, which was 'so encompassing and intense,' now seemed like possessiveness or control, and Emily's independence now seemed like coldness. So what happened? Each was attracted to qualities in the other that they needed to develop in themselves.

This is the irony in one common relationship story. We are often attracted to people who have qualities opposite from those we have. We are attracted to our opposite self. This type of attraction allows us to develop different parts of ourselves. Differences invite people to grow. When you see in your partner qualities very different from your own, you can either criticize or admire the differences.

The choice then, is *grow or blame*. You can grow your partner's qualities in yourself, or you can whine and complain about them in your partner and get caught in 'deadlock' (Trafford, 1982). 'Deadlock' refers to the period of emotional impasse you experience after you fall out of love. Deadlock is when you as a couple are merged instead of being two separate people, and each of you is stuck in automatic, unproductive patterns. In deadlock, for instance, one of you keeps dominating, and the other keeps acting submissive, and no real interaction can occur. You are stuck. You are at a stalemate. Wedlock goes into deadlock, or dreadlock.

This is the point at which couples either break up, or start to live parallel lives, or suddenly get together in a whole new way. Each of you becomes assertive, not submissive or dominating.

You may be wondering why we are talking about relationship dynamics when you are *already divorced*. We discuss falling in and out of love because couples often divorce when they are out of love, or when one partner is at this stage. You are critical of each other's differences and feel that you have to defend your right to be you. You may feel that your partner 'prevents' you from being you. You may feel that *you have to leave or you will die*. Or one of you may feel like this, while the other feels unfairly accused. In either case, you are in a power struggle.

Loss of Love

There are some couples who separate with relief, but they are few. Most couples feel devastated when they have to go separate ways. For many, there aren't enough words to describe the pain, torment, and disappointment involved in ending a relationship. The loss of love can mire you in self-doubt. You worry about your lovability and about your ability to love, and you feel like a failure.

'If this person who has known me so well does not love me, maybe there is something wrong with me,' said Judy, who thought she would never get over the shock of her eight-year marriage ending. She joined a group and was surprised how many felt just the same.

Sometimes people act as though you should 'get over' it in just a few months, as if people are easily replaced. But we are not. As humans we become attached, and when we do, we connect with intense longings. We want our relationships to last forever, and the force of our attachments makes breaking up very hard to do. Even if you wanted to break up, *breaking up is hell*. According to one father, it is 'like a near-death experience.'

> You swing between euphoria, violent rage, and depression. You may become promiscuous and drink too much. At some point, everyone coming out of a marriage mutters to what was once the other half, 'I could kill you.' (Trafford, 1982)

You go through what Abigail Trafford (1982) calls 'crazy time,' acting and feeling as if you are caught in someone else's nightmare or soap opera. You feel, temporarily, out of your mind, and often disconnected from your body. You either cannot slow down, or you are so slowed down that you can't get up. 'Crazy times' takes many forms, but the pain is the same.

How to Cope with the Loss of Love

When you are breaking up, *don't blame yourself or your partner.* Just remember that loving is a learned skill. You cannot 'get it right' right off the bat; it takes practice. We grow and evolve in our ability to love and be loved. For very good reasons, you have ended your relationship; or if it is your partner who has left, you have no choice but to accept that it is over. If you have been left, you need to explore how being with someone who did not commit to you is about some part of your story. If you are the one leaving, you must understand your deeper reasons. In any case, if you stay open to learning all that you can about yourself – about who you are and what you need – you will find a better fit next time. *But only if you handle this break-up with love and maturity.* Ironically, you cannot get over your divorce until you understand what happened in your marriage – until you understand how your *own* (childhood) story got expressed, redone, or undone in your marriage.

> You get over divorce by confronting the kind of relationship there was in your marriage. You realize there aren't any victims. You both recog-

nize your own complicity in the breakup. Then you learn to carry on a relationship that works. (Trafford, 1982)

You get over your marriage by going back *into* it, at least in your mind. By reflecting, analysing, and understanding that the break-up was neither your partner's fault nor your own. It was co-created. There was an unconscious dialogue between you, under the verbal one, that you must learn to understand in order to move on. When you blame yourself or your spouse, you undermine your ability to learn from your experience. It is better to learn from experience than to repeat it.

> *You can get a quickie divorce in Las Vegas, but you cannot get a quickie emotional divorce.*

You do not have to be in love to feel devastated when your partner leaves you. Couples are often surprised at their distress. They are also amazed at how long the grieving takes: 'I just did not expect to feel so bad, for so long, with no let-up. It feels like death.'

PHILOSOPHY OF LIFE

Enduring the loss of love and family as you know it is very difficult. It helps if you have a philosophy or belief system to help you make sense of things. You need a way of thinking, or attitude, that lends meaning to your pain and helps you avoid bitterness. Some use spirituality, religion, psychology, a humanistic philosophy, or a moral code as a means for keeping centred during difficult times.

Whatever philosophy you choose has to allow for learning from mistakes, and for resolving hate, blame, and resentment. Being told to 'forget about it' or 'keep a stiff upper lip' does not foster reflection. It is only as you reflect on your experiences, and learn from them, that you make peace with yourself.

Roman's wife suddenly left him for another man. He was angry and wanted revenge. By badmouthing his wife, he turned his 8-year-old daughter, Tammy, against her. Then one day he heard her in her room crying for her mother. He wanted to bawl her out. Instead, he stopped and reflected. He reflected on her unhappiness and realized that she needed her mother. Because he was angry at her mother, he had assumed Tammy was, too. He set up a meeting for her with her mother.

His daughter was so happy that he wondered why he had not done it sooner. He felt mean. What had hardened his heart? Again, instead of focusing on how mean he had been, he reflected. He remembered witnessing a terrible fight between his parents during which his father accused his mother of having affairs. He remembered how sad and confused he felt at the time. He had not known what to make of it. He had only been 6. Roman saw that he was acting like his angry father, and resolved to change his ways.

No Rituals for Divorce

When you consider how many rituals we have to help couples marry, it is remarkable there aren't any for helping them divorce. Getting married is just one long party – the engagement, white dress, showers, presents, dowry, religious and civil ceremonies, and so on. Yet when couples separate, there is nothing but embarrassment. On top of that the only social institution dedicated to divorce is the legal system. When you are almost out of your mind with emotions, the last thing you need is the legal system.

Criticism of Friends and Loss of Social Supports

Losing a spouse or parent through death is often compared to losing one through separation, but they are very different situations. Children who lose a parent through death show better adjustment than children of divorce (Amato & Keith, 1991). We reflect on the possible reasons for this. A child who loses a parent through death cherishes that parent's memory and carries it inside with the support of the other parent. The child is sad, but not conflicted. After all, he has not lost the father that lives in his mind. He continues to share that father with his mother and relatives.

In a high-conflict separation, the child cannot hold on to the good image of one or both of his parents. When you denigrate each other, you destroy your child's internal daily memory of you both. As a result, the child can feel empty inside. It is almost as if the conflict had killed off one or both of the parents inside him.

Moreover, when a parent dies, the bereaved are offered sympathy and comfort. Usually, families that separate do *not* get much support. Instead, they can feel as if they have done something wrong, or failed in some way. Friends and family do not tolerate the expression of emotions that is so necessary.

One mother put it this way: 'Four months after the separation, my closest friend said, "You're not going to talk about THAT again, are you? When are you going to get over it?"' Others talk of how friends try to match them with dates.

People may be unsupportive or critical because your separation makes them anxious about their own relationships. They may feel threatened. They may not understand family tensions and blame you for not trying hard enough.

Hetherington et al. (1978) report that friends and relatives offer support for *the first three months* after separation. After that it falls off rapidly. An invisible wall suddenly separates 'his' friends and relatives from 'hers.' Those who stay involved usually connect to only one of you. Friends and relatives seem to find it impossible to manage closeness with both of you.

This 'invisible wall' may be the result of how couples use their friends and relatives for comfort during hard times. Separating spouses malign each other as a way to 'get over' their pain. They say awful things about each other and gain relief in doing so. Friends may not understand this, and think that everything you say about your spouse is the whole truth. They are ready to 'take your side' and put your ex down as well. New partners may feel they have to defend you. This may help you feel better for a time, but in the long run, it won't. Taking sides fuels the flames of hostility. It can lead to 'tribal warfare' (Johnston & Campbell, 1988) – a war between each parent's relatives and supporters.

Think back to your friends or relations who divorced. Have you been able to stay close to both sides?

Georgette talked to Cathy every few nights and really appreciated her sup-
port. Cathy made her feel understood. She could complain about Jack, whom
she had left five months earlier. She regaled her with the ups and downs of
their break-up, and always felt relieved after the calls. Once, when Cathy
was visiting, Georgette's daughter, Tina, talked about her father in a very
positive way. Cathy looked confused. Georgette suddenly realized that her
daily diatribes about Jack had turned her friend against him. Although it
may have helped her, she did not want this to hurt Tina. She did not want it
to affect Tina's love for her father.

You need to invest in your friends because you need their support.
Parents with supportive friends and relatives adjust better. Because
you are in a crisis, you have to teach your friends how to help you.
They don't always know what you need. So tell them, or give them
this book.

Redefining your social groupings is another source of stress. Separated couples experience loneliness. Fathers who are alone with
weekend access find that they do not fit in with either the married
crowd or the single crowd. They are caught between two worlds.
When their children are with them, they don't fit with their single
friends. When they are alone, being with families or married couples
feels awkward. Mothers, too, complain that friends worry about
them being 'single,' as if they might steal their husbands.

Jennifer complained, 'Since my divorce, my married girlfriends make me
feel like I'm after their husbands. I get the feeling they think I'm pining for
another man. It's kind of insulting.'

Divorce puts you under stress, which makes it harder for you to deal
with the really crucial issues: taking good care of your children,
yourself, your former spouse, and the new parenting plan for the
care of your children.

FINANCIAL STRESS

The economic downside of divorce has been widely discussed. It is a tragedy that with all the emotional burdens of separating, one of the additional problems – sometimes greatest problem – is that it depletes the family's financial resources. And the economic burden falls more heavily on women and children. On the average, women experience a 15 to 30 per cent decline in their standard of living (Cherlin & Andrew, 1981; Ahrons, 1994). Some men also see a decline in their standard of living; others see a 10 to 15 per cent *increase* in their income. Moreover, until recently, a very large percentage of mothers did not receive their child support payments, and when they did, they did not receive the full amount. The new child support guidelines and the stronger measures by governments to coerce these payments are intended to address this injustice (see Chapter 11).

Since children usually still live with their mothers, it is children who suffer the most from this economic hardship. Just as children need to be close to both parents in order to reach their potential, they also need both parents' financial resources. It is expensive to raise children, and even more expensive when parents separate. This is one of the hidden costs of divorce: two households cost more to support than one. Women still earn two-thirds of what men earn. And yet some parents still withhold child support payments. It is as if some think they are punishing their spouses by withholding support. Yet it is painfully clear that it is children who suffer the most from tightened finances. It is the quality of their lives that suffers (Hodges et al, 1979, as cited in Amato & Keith, 1991). To reach their potential, children need good neighbourhoods, good education, good child care, good nutrition, and so on. Whatever the reason for the fighting over resources, children are penalized when one parent becomes the financial casualty of the separation.

3. Loss of Full-Time Parenting

In this chapter we will examine the second great loss you endure when you divorce: the loss of full-time parenting. We will start by examining this loss and then propose some ways to handle it.

The biggest problem in divorce is that you can never live together again as a family. Although this is an obvious point, it is amazing how hidden it is in disputes. Each parent acts as though he or she could, or should, have the child all the time. As if it were possible. Divorce means that for the rest of your lives, you will have to share your children. Neither of you will ever be a full-time parent again. When you were together as a family, both of you could be with your children all the time because you shared a home. When you wanted to see your child, there was no need to make decisions, no plan to make. Both of you could be 'with your children' all the time. But when you separate, your child's time with you always excludes the other parent. Neither of you will ever again have the child all to yourself. Although parents rarely admit they want their children all to themselves, it is a fairly universal feeling. When parents live together, that desire is easily fulfilled.

In a similar way, when families live together they 'hold' each other's history. As parents you hold the history of your children. You discuss and check these histories with each other, especially around milestones such as weddings, birthdays, and graduations. Thus, 'Do you remember when ...?' The knowledge that parents hold our histories is a comfort to us even when we are adults. This is often what we mourn at the death of a parent: we are alone with our memories. When you separate, you lose this sense of shared time.

Another loss is that of the biological connection. As biological parents, you share a close bond in sharing a child: 'He or she is my flesh and blood.' Sometimes parents feel that no other partner will have the same attachment to a child, because that person will not be the child's biological parent. If you feel like this, you have to mourn this loss.

Children often feel this loss of the biological connection. They realize they are centered in the biology of the family. Children always want to know and stay connected with their biological parents. If children do not know their biological parents, they often seek them out later. This is important to remember. Parents who try to exclude each other from their child's life are often surprised to discover much later that the grown child has sought out and developed a relationship with the extruded parent.

What Is It Like to Parent Separately?

Separating parents have a lot of adjustments to make. They must deal with their personal reactions to their losses. At the same time, they must make adjustments in their parenting style, accept the loss of full-time parenting, get used to parenting alone, find ways to keep the children close to both parents, and handle administrative tasks.

Because of their losses, parents must work through a kaleidoscope of emotions: sadness, a sense of personal failure, anger, temporary losses of competence and self-esteem, and a profound loneliness. It is an enormous transition to be alone as a parent. The stress involved can trigger physical symptoms such as high blood pressure and sleep interruptions, or psychiatric symptoms such as depression and anxiety. Most parents feel unsettled and 'volatile,' weepy and 'not themselves.' These are normal, albeit painful, reactions to the losses they are learning to endure.

These personal reactions make it even harder for you to adjust to your new role as a separated parent. It is hard to get used to the time you must spend away from your children. Some parents say they pine for their children. They miss the day-to-day contact, and dislike having to watch their children come and go.

One mother said, 'I feel lost when the kids aren't with me. I just walk around the house in a daze. I don't feel okay until they get back. How long will this take?'

These difficulties lead to changes in how parents treat their children. Research (Hetherington et al., 1978) shows that right after separating, parents are less competent with their children than they were before the separation. For a while, parents withdraw emotionally from their children, as if they're protecting themselves. Parents become less tuned to their children – more permissive, and more focused on activities as opposed to creative play, stories, and chatting. Or parents may become more demanding and less empathic toward their children. Mothers, especially, may find it hard to manage their sons. They may be stricter with them, and more likely to use the command mode: 'Do this ... do that ...' These temporary deteriorations in parenting style disappear after two or three years, when parents regain their sense of well-being.

Coping with Distressed Kids

Some of your difficulties managing your children after the separation are due not only to your own stress, but also to the fact that your children are stressed and distressed. Suddenly, you have very upset and demanding children on your hands. Children show many regressed and aggressive behaviours during this time because they are shocked and horrified when their parents separate. Upset children demand extra care and nurturing. They need a considerable amount of parental care to offset the terrible fears they are experiencing. These fears are called 'separation anxiety.' Separation anxiety can be defined as an intense fear of losing, or becoming separated from, someone you love (Bowlby, 1982). Separation anxiety is the feeling that your world is falling apart. Children perceive the break-up to their parents as a catastrophe of that magnitude. Children in the grip of these fears are agitated, depressed, and hard to comfort. They need to be reassured that you love them and that they won't be left like you are leaving each other. They need to be reassured about the security of their connection to both of you, because you are their rock and their foundation. This is very taxing for you to deal with, especially when you yourself are going through such a hard time.

'Tommy has always been a calm, well-mannered little boy, but since we separated, he is a lion. He just doesn't stop: demanding, wanting, and worst of all, following me around. Yes, I know why he is doing this, but it doesn't make it any easier to take. Sometimes when I leave work, instead of going straight home, I stop off at Starbucks and sit down with a coffee to catch my breath, because I know what is awaiting me when I get there.'

Being a separated parent is stressful. It is very different from being a live-in parent sharing the child care tasks. Even if you are reconciled to the decision to separate, and relieved to be free of your marriage, you miss the support of another parent in the home. You miss the time-out you give each other when the going gets tough.

In most families, parents rely heavily on each other in caring for the children. You share the fetch-and-carry of their physical needs. You use each other as a check and balance as you try to respond to your children's changing needs. In an ongoing dialogue ('duologue'), you discuss and evaluate their personalities, strengths, and vulnerabilities. You try to discuss the different stages they are going through, and help each other adjust to them. You try to balance each other off, give each other 'time out,' act as each other's consultant and support, and compensate for each other's deficits. You also recruit the help of your families and friends.

Staying a Parental Team

You must not lose this sense of teamwork when you separate. The investment you both have in the well-being of your children is an asset worth protecting. Continue to act like a team: 'What would his father think of this?' 'How would her mother handle this problem? I should check with her.' Even when neither of you feels like part of a team, it is best to act like one. There will be times when this is really hard. Because you are the only adult in the home with the children, and because you may still be angry with the other parent, you may start acting like you are the *only* parent.

It takes a real effort not to think you are the only parent or that the other parent's opinion is not as important as yours. There will be days when not consulting with the other parent feels like a great short cut, but too many short cuts will shut him out. Including the other parent is not always easy, and *thoughtful inner dialogues* are often necessary to bring you around.

Geraldine reflected, 'Why should I include him in all the decisions I make for Joey? Half the time I can't even get him on the phone, so I have to hang around waiting. Like when I was registering Joey for summer camp, and I forgot which dates his father was taking him on vacation. I just felt like winging it, but if I got it wrong, it would be a hassle. Looking back on it now, I'm glad I checked because Joey would have hated to miss his two-week holiday with his dad. And yet sometimes, it is such a hassle to include him. Why? It takes a lot of extra work, and to be honest, I'm still so mad that he left me in this mess. At these times I get mad and think, "Why should I sweat for him and his good times with the kids? Why should I include him? He wasn't there when we needed him, why should I make him there now?" Then I tell myself how much fun Joey has with him and I try to let it go.

'The same thing occurs around Joey's problems. In the last six months, Joey has been doing badly at school, and I'm worried about it. It was hard to bring it up with Bill because I was afraid he would blame me for Joey's difficulty. After all, Joey lives with me during the school week. But I'm glad I did, because Bill had many good ideas about what he and I could do. We now have a joint plan of action and I don't feel so alone. It's funny how I always think I should manage alone, and then when Bill helps I feel so much better. Bringing up kids is a lot of responsibility, and I feel less burdened when we share it emotionally as well as physically.'

Keeping Children Close to Both of You

To keep the children closely connected to both of you takes joint, dedicated effort. In the case of very young children, extra-special efforts are needed to connect the child to his father because of how that particular relationship develops in the family. In many families, babies begin their lives by being very close to the mother. This is probably because mothers carry children and – although this is slowly changing – are more likely to stay home with the children for the first few months or years. Besides, newborns and very young children need a secure attachment with mainly one parent. A baby's sense of security depends strongly on the presence of that person, who, as just stated, is usually the mother.

Because of this attachment, mothers have a powerful position in the minds and hearts of children. As the infant grows and develops, he becomes aware of other people in his environment, like his father and his siblings. Most particularly, he notices the special relationship between his parents. This predisposes him to look expectantly and lovingly to his father, with whom he also bonds in a very special attachment.

When families separate, the question is how to help younger children gravitate toward the father (or the other parent), when he is not as much a part their daily environment as the mother. To compensate for this lack of daily contact, finely tuned co-operation is required. As the father (or the other parent), you must take pains to establish a strong emotional connection with your younger child. This 'getting to know you' stage takes considerable attentiveness. Infants need you to be at their disposal. They have to be number one.

As the mother (or the residential parent), you need to make special efforts to support and maintain your child's closeness to the other parent. Because younger children cannot handle much disruption in routines or extended time away from you, times with the father must be short and frequent. But between visits, you can encourage their relationship by talking warmly to your child about father, by displaying his photos, and by treating him warmly in the child's presence.

After a two-year marriage, George and Anne separated amicably when Wendy was one year old. They attended counselling to create 'a good divorce' – a difficult achievement. After heated discussions and much tooing and froing, they began to grieve their losses. George felt devastated that he could not live with Wendy. Anne wept for the end of her marriage. In time, they sold their small house and rented apartments close to each other and the pre-school Wendy would be attending. They divided Wendy's toys and belongings so that she would feel at home in both places. Because of her age, Wendy spent more time with her mother, but the parents created a schedule that allowed Wendy to get used to her father in small enough time frames that she was able to maintain the security of her connection to her mother. After work, her father picked her up on Tuesdays and Thursdays for the evening. On Saturday mornings her mother brought Wendy to her father's, where she stayed until the early afternoon. On Sundays for two hours, George took Wendy to the park.

George was very sensitive to those times when Wendy suddenly expressed a need for her mother. He would at those times return her to her mother and spend a little more time with her. Or if Wendy did not settle, he would leave her with her mother. Even though he was sorry to cut short his time with her, George took Wendy back to her mother.

George and Anne intend to expand Wendy's time with her father as she gets older.

Not all parents manage this degree of good will. Many find they cannot separate without anger and resentment. This is understandable, and part of the grieving. Even amicable couples have the greatest number of fights during this period. Here is the problem: most parenting plans are laid down in the first few months after separation. Research shows that those plans change little throughout the child's life (Maccoby & Mnookin 1992; Ahrons, 1994). It is ironic that parents are most likely to fight just at the point in their child's life when co-operation is most necessary. This is an important point, which must be managed well.

Patrick loved his time with his 5-year-old daughter, Tammy. He looked forward to their weekends. Tammy, however, was going through a very insecure time about her place in her mother's affections, and wanted to sleep at her mother's every Friday night, although this was her time with her father. At first, Patrick opposed the idea of her going home, because 'this was my time with Tammy.' But when Tammy cried every Friday, he was moved by her distress and took her home as she asked. Tammy could not explain her reasons. She told her father she had 'certain feelings in her head' that made her need her mother. When she returned from these visits home, she was very warm and affectionate with her father. Although he hated breaking up his weekend, Patrick came to see that he was doing what Tammy needed, and he relaxed into her wishes.

Patrick is a very wise parent. There are times when children require special favours, or preferred treatment that on the surface seems strange or irrational. In these situations it is best to follow the child's lead even if you don't quite understand what is happening. The deeper reasons will reveal themselves in time.

Another factor that needs special attention when you separate is a child's periodic longing for one or the other parent. Your children have different relationships with each of you, not just because each of you is unique and special, but because of your different genders. Children are sensitive to these differences and will sometimes gravitate more toward one parent than the other. It is important to allow for this. For instance, an infant boy may want to spend all his time with his mother, and may cry helplessly for her when he needs comforting. However, the same little boy, when he is 3, may long to be only with his dad.

Administrative Tasks

In addition to these emotional tasks, as separated parents you have many administrative tasks to complete. You have to settle the legal separation, the division of property and assets, and the parenting plan. As well, you often have to change residences, schools, and sometimes work. You also have to inform family, friends, and colleagues at work of changes in the family, and comfort them as necessary. With everything you have to do together, you simply cannot make a clean break from each other, even if it is just what you may need (at least for a short time).

What You Need Most When You Are Separating: Self-Care

When you are separating, the most important thing you can do is take kind and knowledgable care of yourself. Everything depends on you being in good shape. Realize that you are going through a trauma, a crisis that is shaking your foundations. Although your first impulse may be to run away, or get busy to distract yourself from the pain, or get romantically involved, we would recommend the opposite. Slow down, breathe deeply, and let yourself experience your distress and whatever feelings you are experiencing. *You will feel many feelings, and they will pass, but only if you let yourself feel them.* Don't be afraid of your distress, and don't fight it. You *will* feel better, but not for some time.

Resist all temptations to avoid grieving. Tell your friends that you will be unhappy for a while. Teach them to *listen*, but without problem solving – you need an ear, not advice. Sometimes friends need to be taught how to help us. Tell your friends to just go 'hmm ... hmm ...' while you do all the talking. Tell them you will return the favour when they need it.

Don't isolate yourself, even if you are tempted to do so. It is no wonder you want to isolate yourself when you are upset. Our society has low tolerance for the painful emotions that occur after events like death and divorce. People often avoid you when you are upset. And when they are with you some try to close you off from your pain. 'Be strong,' 'Don't cry,' and so on are warnings for you to hide your sorrow and distress. These warnings promote a view of life that discourages you from developing your inner life. By taking serious care of your emotional life, you are helping yourself get through the bad times as quickly as possible.

Some friends, no matter how much you direct them to listen, will simply be unable to tolerate your distress. Don't spend time with them right now. Instead, spend time with those who can handle the emotional state you are in, and who can listen. You owe it to yourself and to your family to surround yourself with emotional support.

Find a support group or a therapist who can help you understand the causes of your separation. This will pave the way for better communication with your ex (see the appendix for help in choosing a therapist). Get guidance and support for your new role as a single parent. Don't blame or denigrate your ex *or* yourself: it won't help.

Be sad, not mad. Learn to tolerate your sad, mad, and bad feelings. Sit with them. Avoiding them will make you blame. Don't blame yourself or your ex. Try to learn from what happened and leave it behind.

4. The Separating Process

As we said earlier, separating is a long complicated *process*. It starts with the crisis of the family breaking up, and evolving from a single family structure to a two-unit family. As the family adjusts to the new structure, it faces many pressures. Each member undergoes stress, but at different times and in different ways.

THE CRISIS OF THE SEPARATION

Usually, long before the decision to separate, you are unhappy with each other. When you quarrel, you cannot support each other or act as a team. ('Things just fell apart,' is the way Nancy described this period.) This unhappiness is expressed in hot or cold wars. Hot wars are the yelling and the screaming. In cold wars the silence is deafening. Research shows that how parents handle their family before the separation is just as important to children's adjustment as how they handle the divorce (Elliot & Richards, 1991, as cited in Kelly, 1993). The same study made it clear that many children with adjustment problems after the divorce had symptoms of those problems before the divorce.

Four-year-old Kelly always remembered the 'shouting in my ear,' which went on for months before her parents separated. She went to bed with pillows over both ears to block out the noise. She then started shouting to herself to get over the sound. Sometimes she did this when there was no shouting, just because she got used to it.

A Great Way to Handle the Decision to Separate

It is much better for children if you can agree to separate and work out a joint plan. It is worse when you separate because of a sudden, explosive event. It is terrible for children when you can only manage to separate by being horrible to each other. Children become frightened. Parents often believe that their children can differentiate between their parents' nastiness toward each other from their feelings toward their children. But children cannot tell the difference: 'If Mommy treats Daddy like this when she is mad, how will she treat me when she's mad at me?' Children do not interpret your behaviour or try to make sense of it: they just get hurt. Your children need you to be neutral with each other, at least in front of them. When you are civilized with each other, you foster your children's sense of security with both of you. When one of you yells at the other, it undermines your children's connection to both of you, and their confidence in you.

Six-year-old David said it best: 'He yelled at her, she yelled at him. My heart stopped and I can't stop remembering it.' Now I keep worrying that they will yell at me.'

A teenager put it this way: 'Why should I believe she'll always love me? I saw how she treated my father, and she certainly loved him once, too. I feel I have to be on my best behaviour or else.'

The following is an excellent way to separate.

When the Smiths wanted to separate, they attended counselling. Although the divorce was clearly Ms Smith's decision, for the children's sake they talked about the decision to separate as a mutual decision. They brought the children to the interviews. Each child sat close to a parent. The parents told their children they would not continue to live together 'because we do not love each other like we used to. We fight a lot. We have decided that Daddy will move out of the house into an apartment of his own.' Here, 7-year-old Rachel threw herself into her mother's arms and cried. 'Why don't you love each other? What happened?' She yelled at them 'to try harder, try harder.'

The parents continued, 'Although we don't love each other the way we used to, we will always love you ... Sometimes parents separate from each other, but parents never separate from their children.' Rachel collapsed in tears, and her younger brother climbed off his father's lap to comfort her. She expressed anger and grief on and off for many months.

When parents separate the way the Smiths did, children manage better. They stay emotionally connected to you. And because you aren't using up your energy fighting, you can be attentive to them. When couples separate in volatile, violent, or dramatic ways, divorce easily escalates into high conflict. One parent attacks, and the other retaliates, and a vicious circle begins.

Who Decides to Separate?

The decision to separate is rarely mutual. There is usually one leaving and one being left. While both positions are painful, they are different. The decision to separate often comes from the *woman*. Wallerstein and Kelly (1980) and Ahrons (1994) noted that approximately three-quarters of the time, the woman left her husband. Women feel the pain of separation before it happens because they think about it and turn it over in their minds. They may be more prepared for the separation, but they carry the greater guilt for the decision: 'He just never noticed how bad things were between us, so I had to make the decision to separate. But then I'm left wondering, "Was I being too hard on him? Could we have worked things out?"' The one who makes the decision has more doubts about it.

When the separation is imposed on you, you feel disempowered, abandoned, and helpless. You may feel as if the tables have been turned on you: 'I had no idea she was unhappy. She never said anything. I did not have a chance to do anything about it. I could have changed things. This way, I feel I had no say and I feel very resentful about it.'

Managing Your Anger with Your Ex

The clearer you are that your relationship is over, the sooner you will adjust. The stronger your attachment to your ex, the more you fight and the harder it is to grieve and let go. Being intense and hostile is a sign that you are still strongly attached. *The opposite of love is not hate, but detachment.*

Managing your anger with your ex is your biggest challenge. Assume you are angry, even if you do not feel it. Many people complain about their spouse's anger but ignore their own. Understanding that you are angry allows you to manage it. Anger is an emotion that requires careful handling, especially when it comes to the other parent.

This is not to say you should *not* be angry: yes you should. Your anger will eventually push you to where you need to go. Constructive anger will help you discover what you need and where to get it. You *need* to be angry, and you *need* to be aware of your anger, and you should express it in a safe place. With your spouse is not a safe place for you to express your anger.

When parents become aware of their anger, they feel frightened and overwhelmed and want rules and guidelines to handle it. Rules are a very good idea, because your anger is short term (although it may not feel like it) whereas your relationship with the other parent is long term. You want to act in ways that protect your relationship.

We recommend caution: some things should never be said, and some things can never be unsaid. It is important not to say things that will inflame your partner. Anger has an obsessional quality: in the middle of the night, people remember terrible things that were said, and their hearts turn to stone.

The free expression of anger is not recommended in most relationships. Some very successful, long-term, intimate relationships can tolerate and even get over expressed anger. But generally relationships are not well served by angry outbursts. Human beings are fragile and often jockey for self-esteem. We are not good at handling frontal attacks. We either collapse under fire or shoot back from the lip. Neither helps. To decrease your anger takes intelligence, self-awareness, and savvy. This is a lot to keep in your mind, especially when you are bent out of shape with rage.

Better to take the moderate road – the one where you stay civilized and spare yourself and your family the ugliness of uncontrolled behaviour. Civilized discussions, with generous sprinklings of the 'I' word, are much safer. For instance, saying 'I get angry when you are late and don't call' will get you farther than yelling, 'You are always late. You don't care about us !'

Besides, it is quite possible that anger has already eroded much of the trust between you. Both of you have probably said things that you will one day wish had been left unsaid (though not necessarily now). You need to find a way of rebuilding trust. So don't express your anger to each other. Retread yourselves instead as 'business partners': partners in the business of rearing children. There is no place for free-wheeling anger in business relationships.

Don't react to your ex-partner. 'Reacting' means your ex is in charge of your buttons. 'Responding' means *you* are in charge. Think before replying!

So what can you do with the anger you can't afford to unload on the other parent? You sit with it, look at it, taste it, until eventually you understand it. That's the good news about anger: it teaches you about yourself, or the situation. It won't harm you to contain it. Talk to a friend or therapist. Keep a journal. Write letters to your ex, but don't mail them, just study them. What is the real target of your anger? When you recognize what you feel, you are in control of yourself and able to hold your fire. Real power comes from self-management.

Grieving is not pleasant, but it does have its positive side. As mental health professionals know, grieving promotes emotional strength. It allows you to proceed to new stages in your development and to survive life's difficulties and crises. It helps you 'to get over it,' 'to move on.' Dealing with loss allows you to resolve painful feelings that would otherwise interfere with your ability to handle future problems. Grieving requires maturity and integrity. Some people cannot grieve, and use psychotherapy to learn how to grieve. Most therapies create a safe place for people to express painful and uncomfortable feelings.

Some people have personality styles that are too rigid to allow for grieving; these people simply find it too difficult to connect to their vulnerabilities. This is unfortunate because many experiences in close relationships require openness to feelings. Those who can experience grief are able to more fully experience intimacy, joy, and fulfilment.

When separated parents cannot grieve, they quarrel, resort to custody and access disputes, and block shared parenting. They resort to compulsive and hostile behaviours. For a short time, right after the separation, many parents are unhelpful to each other; this is so common as to almost be expected. However, when nastiness and hostility between parents becomes prolonged, and their conflict involves the children, it threatens the separated family's well-being. Parents and children who can endure the four stages of mourning will eventually achieve 'a good divorce.'

Jim loved Sarah and could not accept that she left him. He started drinking to excess and smoking marijuana. He withdrew from his children, who eventually asked not to see him, because they were frightened by his moods. When his wife took him to court for putting the children at risk through his out-of-control behaviours, the penny dropped. He realized that the drinking and the toking were not going to bring Sarah back or help him dull the pain. They would only cause him to lose his children, in addition to his wife. Fear motivated him to deal with his loss.

HOW TO GRIEVE YOUR LOSSES

After any significant loss, you go through four stages of emotional response: *numbness and denial, yearning and protest, disorganization and despair,* and *reorganization and reintegration* (Bowlby, 1980). These stages are illustrated on the accompanying diagram. They may occur in sequence, or out of sequence, or as a jumble. They are similar to the five stages that follow the death of a loved one – stages that Elizabeth Kübler-Ross (1969) described in her well-known book, *On Death and Dying.* She labelled them: *denial, anger, bargaining, depression* and *acceptance.*

THE GRIEVING PROCESS

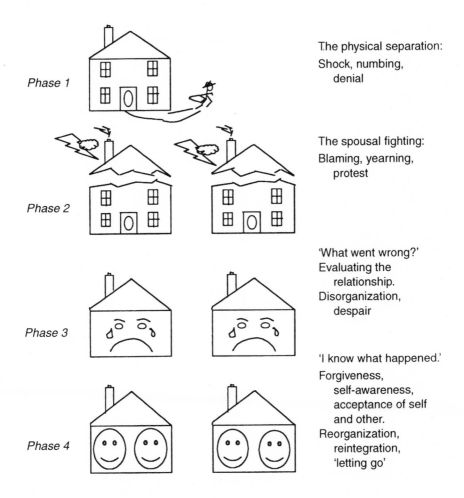

Phase 1

The physical separation:
Shock, numbing,
    denial

Phase 2

The spousal fighting:
Blaming, yearning,
    protest

Phase 3

'What went wrong?'
Evaluating the
    relationship.
Disorganization,
    despair

Phase 4

'I know what happened.'
Forgiveness,
    self-awareness,
    acceptance of self
    and other.
Reorganization,
    reintegration,
    'letting go'

H. McDonough, MSW, CSW, 1997

1. Numbness and Denial

The most basic early response to loss is denial. Denial of sorrow is why you are able to manage the funeral of a loved one, but then suddenly collapse two weeks later. In a separation, denial often starts when one of you asks for a divorce or he leaves the house. You know he won't be back, but you wait anyway. You should know better, but you don't, because your mind is racing ahead, coming up with reasons why he will be back. You just wait, immobilized. You are in shock, you are in denial: 'This is not happening.'

When you first realized you had problems in your marriage, you probably denied them, saying to yourself, 'It's not really that bad. I'm just seeing it worse than it is. It will look different in the morning.' A little later, you may have admitted that you had some problems, but you probably minimized their importance: 'Well yeah, we haven't had sex for months and months but that doesn't mean anything ...' It was only slowly that it really dawned on you: 'We have problems.' Then you started looking at them.

The denial phase usually lasts a few months, sometimes longer. It is not unusual for it to come and go over time. While you are in denial, it is difficult to make plans. Some people, by temperament, are more likely to deny problems than others. In this phase, some separated parents still live together 'for the sake of the children.' Although this rarely works out in the long term, it gives you some recovery time.

2. Yearning and Protest

Losing a close relationship brings on feelings such as yearning, anger, and protest. *Yearning*, an acutely painful state, means wishing things could be as you hoped – for instance, wishing you had stayed in love. Losing the other person is so painful that some parents promise anything to persuade their partner to stay. Some deal with yearning by clinging to children, parents, friends, and religion.

Anger comes when wishing does not work. It is not what you wished ... it is over and ... you are angry. Anger is an uncomfortable feeling to endure and contain. People often 'dump' their anger on those around them. *Protest* includes anger, rage, resentment, and loss of control. In the anger phase, parents become obsessed with thoughts of revenge. Blaming maintains anger, and often covers guilt and sadness.

3. *Disorganization and Despair*

Marital breakdown leads to personal disorientation: that is, a sense of being lost, confused, and desperate. A family and intimate relationship provide security, safety, and a sense of identity. Take that away, and who are you? You must redefine yourself. Because old patterns of thinking, feeling, and acting must be endured before new ones can take their place, you usually feel worse before you get better. You become depressed and listless. Disorientation and despair are unpleasant, but they are a normal part of grieving that you just have to endure.

Some parents are unable to endure these feelings. They try to relieve them in destructive ways. The most common are aggression, fighting with family members, and compulsive behaviours like overwork, overspending, and abusing alcohol and drugs. These activities serve to take your mind off the pain it cannot manage.

4. *Reorganization and Reintegration*

Divorce, whether chosen or imposed, can be a chance for a new beginning – for a new way of being, a new way of thinking, new plans, and new attitudes. It can be the time you choose to start living more in tune with yourself.

As Michael reflected, 'When we got divorced, I thought that just about anything that could go wrong did. It is the one thing I most dreaded. My parents were happily married for a century, or so it seemed. For my marriage to fold in eight years ... well, I thought the roof had caved in. And it had. The funny, unexpected thing was that after the cave-in, slowly this other thing started happening. About three years after the separation I started loosening up. I started noticing things again, talking to people, found new interests – some of them weird. Every now and then, I'd pinch myself: "could this be happening to me?" I had been so depressed, I believed I could never rebuild my life. I never though I'd feel good again.

As the feelings associated with grief begin to resolve themselves, you focus on new routines. The need to blame gives way to new choices and opportunities. A new sense of identity emerges: you have survived the despair and are wiser, stronger, safer, and more secure. You are less concerned with the past, and you regain a sense of well-being and hope.

WHAT IS A GOOD DIVORCE?

The term 'the Good Divorce' was popularized by Connie Ahrons in her book by that title (1994). It refers to a divorce in which family bonds are maintained and children's needs are met.

When parents and children are able to proceed through the four stages of grieving, they recover and achieve a good divorce. Some families reject this term because they feel it makes light of the pain of divorce. But the term refers to the 'goodness' of divorce from the child's point of view, not the parents.' A divorce may well be necessary to end a marriage that is damaging the adults, but that divorce should not damage the children. Not all divorces protect kids. Those that do are blame-free, like amicable and disengaged divorces.

Partners have achieved a good divorce when they are able to stop fighting and become a co-operative team, for the sake of the children. That is what is meant by a good divorce. A good divorce offers children the best chance of surviving family dissolution without long-term scars. Two to four years after separation, most families in co-operative divorces regain their former levels of functioning. Children can handle a good divorce better than certain bad marriages. Children *cannot* handle intense parental conflict, either in marriage or in divorce. Good divorces settle those conflicts.

Connie left Jim and took Robert, their 6-year-old. During the marriage, Jim had felt Connie was unhappy but had hoped it would pass. After the separation, Connie avoided Jim, probably out of guilt. Jim was angry and wanted

to confront her, and turned every contact into a quarrel. Connie refused fur-
ther contact, so Jim sent messages through Robert. Robert felt the anger in
the messages and became sad and weary. During the day, he often lay on his
bed with headaches. Robert felt angry that his parents were pulling him into
their fights, but he could not express his anger. He worried that his parents
would be angry with him, and he couldn't even think about them being
angry with him because he felt so alone and isolated.

The couple attended mediation to set up a parenting plan. Connie
described her guilt about having had an affair during their marriage, and
told Jim she was sorry she had hurt him. Jim confessed he had been afraid to
face their marital problems. He realized that his anger was a cover for his
feelings of being betrayed and humiliated. The conflict diminished, and Rob-
ert's vitality returned.

- Grieving your losses allows you to co-operate with your ex-spouse.
- Co-operating leads to a 'good divorce.'
- A good divorce requires even more maturity and self-man-agement than a good marriage. You have to share what is most precious to you, *your child*, with someone you do not like or trust. And share you must, or you'll hurt your child. When your child is with the other parent, you miss her and want to know how she is. You know you should not ask about their time together because that puts her on the spot. So there are gaps in your knowledge of your child's life. You have to let your child go – there are parts of her life that you cannot share. This can be difficult and painful. Sooner or later all parents have to let their children go; separated parents have to let their children go much sooner.

Is a Good Divorce Better Than a Bad Marriage?

Parents often want to be reassured that they did 'the right thing' by divorcing. Most parents have doubts about this now and then. These doubts arise when they face difficulties in the separation. Some separations start with a 'honeymoon phase,' during which everything seems calm and organized. Later, the problems come, and bring doubts: 'Maybe I should have tried harder to save the marriage.' 'Maybe it was not as bad as I thought.'

The following are our reflections on whether a good divorce is better for children than a bad marriage.

1. A somewhat unhappy marriage that does not hurt the children is better for children than a divorce (Wallerstein & Kelly, 1980). Such a marriage may not be satisfying for you, and it may lack intimacy or sexual excitement, but you are good parents together. Children in such marriages are content and happy. If you were to interview them, they would not necessarily be aware of their parents' dissatisfaction. Children are self-centred by nature; they do not notice how their parents are doing unless it is forced upon them. Children take happiness for granted.

2. Provided the conflict remains contained between you, and does not spill over onto the children, a conflicted marriage is better for children than a divorce.

3. A conflicted marriage with the children as the battleground is worse for children than a divorce (Amato & Keith, 1991). In this kind of conflict, the parents use the children against each other.

   This conflicted marriage is likely to become a high-conflict divorce, which is as bad.

Twelve-year-old Shirley was caught in a disagreement between her parents about her education. Should she attend Montessori, as mother wanted, or the local public school, as father wished? If this were really about schools, Shirley would not be hurt. But in this family the conflict about schools is actually covering a power struggle about which parent has the power to make the decision. Shirley's academic and social needs, which should be the foremost criteria, have been displaced by things that have nothing to do with her – that is, the power struggle between her parents.

4. A high-conflict divorce is very damaging to children.

5. Children's Reactions to Divorce

GENERAL REACTIONS

Children are always distressed when their families break up. Research shows that children, unlike adults, do not see separation as a way of improving their lives. When questioned about this later in life, children usually say they wish their parents had stayed together (Wallerstein & Kelly, 1980). In this sense, when it comes to divorce, children see things differently from their parents. Adults divorce in the hope of finding a better partner to live with, as reflected in the high rate of re-marriage (75 per cent of women and 80 per cent of men remarry; Hetherington et al., 1985). Adults can seek to replace those they have lost, whereas children know that their parents are the only biological ones they will ever have: parents are irreplaceable to children. Most children mentioned reduced or lost contact with a parent as the most negative result of divorce (Hetherington et al., 1982; Warshak & Santrock, 1983; Wallerstein & Kelly, 1980).

When a parent leaves the home, the child panics and thinks he is losing everything. The child experiences a terrible loss, a tragedy. The departure of one parent, from the home that was shared by both, raises for the child a natural anxiety about further losses or complete abandonment. This is because children are highly dependent on their parents, and know it and are always afraid to lose them. To lose a parent, or the emotional connection to a parent, is a child's worst fear. This is a biologically encoded fear that threatens all children. It is what makes them afraid of the dark and afraid to be alone. When parents divorce, these primitive fears are brought to the fore.

The family has been the foundation of the child's identity and security. In the family structure, he has felt surrounded and invulnerable. Two adults have been at his disposal and concerned about his well-being. This is the structure he has come to associate with emotional safety – this is 'home.' The loss of it opens for children a painful sense of their own vulnerability. However consistent and predictable, a part-time relationship with a parent cannot replace the intimacy of two parents living together. This adjustment is very difficult, and children must be helped to protest about it. Children who have full and rewarding relationships with both parents can manage these fears better because they are reassured by the constant presence of their parents. These children are less vulnerable to later difficulties.

During the first two years after separation, children develop a variety of problems as they deal with the number of changes associated with divorce. Boys, in particular, can become more difficult to manage. They have more problems in social relationships, and more problem behaviour in school. Many children slip back into less mature behaviour and become clingy, anxious, withdrawn, and sad. They are more dependent, anxious, and depressed. Teachers describe these children as 'dazed,' 'preoccupied,' and lacking concentration. Some children seem withdrawn and stay close to home, unable to invest in outside activities. Children of all ages fantasize that their parents will get back together, which is a way of staving off pain.

Wallerstein (1985) described some children who become sad and dejected as 'overburdened.' This is a very good term because it suggests the load that children carry when they are worried about their parents. When parents are preoccupied with their own difficulties, children become overly tuned to them. They are very distressed by their parents' suffering and want to help.

During the separation of his parents, 8-year-old Gerald was worried that he could not be with both his parents at the same time: 'I'm so sad they can't both have me.' He felt they both needed him. So he thought up a solution. He suggested that he make a Xerox of himself at his father's office: 'He has a huge Xerox machine. I could lie down on it sideways and make a Xerox of myself. The original will go to my mother, and the duplicate to my father.

That way I can take care of both of them, and I won't have to keep worrying about one when I am with the other.'

Children worry when their parents are suffering, and are often in turmoil because of their fears that no one will tend to their needs. There is some justification for these fears. Research (Wallerstein & Kelly, 1980) shows that in the first two years after divorce, children suffer from reduced parental care.

What Influences the Child's Adjustment to the Divorce?

A child's response to divorce is coloured by age, gender, and stage of development at the time of the separation. Other factors are the child's temperament, attitude toward life, social and extended family supports, and extracurricular interests. The child's experience in the family before the divorce, and the adjustment of the parent with whom the child spends the most time, are crucial. The child's experience of his parents' conflict figures very largely in his adjustment. Finally, the nature of his post-divorce relationship with each parent greatly affects his well-being.

What Is Meant by a Child's Temperament?

Temperament greatly affects children's ability to cope. A child's temperament is his innate personality orientation. Some children seem to 'roll with the punches.' Nothing really bothers them, and their parents describe them as children who 'take life as it comes.' They are resilient and flexible, and cope with divorce more easily than children who have more demanding, anxious dispositions. Naturally, the more flexible the child's temperament, the easier the adjustment to divorce.

CHILDREN'S REACTIONS DEPEND ON THEIR AGE

Preschoolers

Children of this age cannot grasp the idea of cause and effect in relationships. To them, everything in the family was wonderful, and then suddenly everything fell apart. They are traumatized. Preschoolers have a very active fantasy life: they 'make life up' as they go along. They actively wish, imagine, and play at reconciling their parents. As well, preschoolers tend to see themselves as central to what happens around them, and to see events only in relation to themselves. In this sense they are by nature 'self' centred. During the separation, for instance, they do not understand that mommy and daddy are leaving each other. They think, 'Daddy left *me*' or 'Mommy left *me*.' They cannot be objective: objectivity develops later in children.

In their play, preschoolers reenact their experience of the separation. They play it out using toys.

In our playroom, Debbie started by having all the family dolls in the playhouse happy and together, and then suddenly she wrecked everything. The dolls and the playhouse went flying. Then she frantically 'forced' the mommy and daddy doll together, putting them together in the bed, at the table, and in the house.

Because preschoolers see themselves as central to events, when a parent moves out of the shared home, they think they did something to alienate that parent. They are anxious and guilty, and therefore work hard at getting their parents back together.

Four-year-old Patrick suggested getting 'a magic cookie' for his mommy and daddy: when they ate it, 'they will love each other again.'

Preschoolers suffer terribly when their parents separate, because they fear they will also be left. In their anxiety, they regress to earlier behaviours to comfort themselves. They suck their thumbs, go back to their favourite teddy bears, and/or masturbate more often. They lose some of their hard-earned competencies, like toilet training.

If you have a preschooler, reassure her over and over that the family disruption was not her fault. Tell her that although the other parent is living elsewhere, he still loves her. Say it in as many ways as you can. It will help her counteract the fears noted above.

When you notice your child trying to help you resolve quarrels with your ex, or trying to distract you from them, stop arguing with your partner. Thank your child for trying to help, and reassure her that it is *your* job, not hers, to stop fighting. Tell her that although you slip at times, you know you can handle it. Tell her you know how hard it is for her to see you fighting and to see you separated. Tell her you will try to keep the fights away from her – and then do it.

Mary asked 4-year-old Joey how he felt when they fought. Joey said it made him 'sad and scared.' He felt he had to bring peace. He felt he had to decide who was right and who was wrong. He was already scared because his parents were not living together any more. He worried all the time that his mother would also leave and he would be all alone. Mary reassured Joey that she and his daddy loved him. She told him his dad was down the street and he would see him tomorrow. She also told Joey he did not have to solve his parents' problems. These were adult issues and he was 'just a kid.' Both parents reassured Joey that he would not lose them.

Put your parenting plan in place, and make sure the children see both of you often. Most of all, *do not fight with each other in front of your preschooler.* They simply cannot handle it – they are already on overload.

School-Age Children

Six- to eight-year-old children tend to be the group most distressed by separation (Amato & Keith, 1991; Wallerstein & Kelly, 1980). Because they are centred on family and home, they are affected by anything that threatens them. These children no longer view themselves as central to events, and do not think they cause things to happen. They have the maturity to understand a little more about relationships, but they do not fully appreciate the dynamics of intimate relationships. They long for their parents to stay together, not because they feel guilty and anxious (like the little ones) but because they know and value what the family means to their own well-being. They experience the tragedy of the loss for themselves, and they are inconsolable.

While listening to a reading of 'The Dinosaurs' Divorce,' and looking at the picture of the dinosaur couple on their wedding day, 6-year-old George said he wished he could 'rewind the tape' back to his parents' wedding and make it all work out. He said he saw a picture of his parents on their wedding day at his grandmother's house, and wept.

When their parents separate, these children are terrified and do all they can to stay connected to both. These children are easily drawn into their parents' conflicts and are very vulnerable to loyalty conflicts.

Eight-year-old Daniel drew a picture of himself. On the right side of his head was the caption 'My daddy is stoopid,' and on the other side was the caption, 'My daddy is not stoopid.' Then he drew fists pounding on both sides of the head. 'I love them both.'

Jennifer confided to her counsellor, 'My mommy doesn't like to see my face happy when I return from my father's.'

Taking sides gives children relief from feeling torn apart. They side with one parent and blame the other. They shift their allegiance from one parent to the other, depending on which one they are with. This is how they stay close to both parents, and although it works for them, it can create confusion and difficulties between you and the other parent. If you feel angry at the other parent, and your 8-year-old comes home telling tales about that parent, be careful not to react to the stories, because they may not be true. Wait till you are no longer angry with the other parent, then see if the child repeats the stories.

Make sure your child expresses his sadness and frustration about your divorce. Ensure that he has consistent time with both of you. Show him the parenting plan – he may even want a copy. Keep contacts with extended family in good repair so that he has a sense of continuity in the midst of the rupture.

Be careful not to denigrate your ex in front of him. If he starts telling you stories about the other parent, ask him how he feels about going back and forth between you. Does he have any suggestions for making things easier for him? Most of all, comfort him, and let him be sad.

Older School-Aged Children

These children have more ego strengths and do not regress like younger children. They put on more of a front to cope with the shock of their parents' separation. They use denial and casualness to hide their fear and pain. Being among older children at school, they are keenly aware of the social context of separation, and tend to feel shame about the family's disruption. Some lie about their situation, and don't tell their friends about the divorce. They are more likely to blame their parents for separating, and to berate them on moral grounds.

Because of these dynamics, children in this age group are more likely to develop more permanent alliances with one parent against the other. Wallerstein & Kelly's research (1980) showed that twice as many children formed an alliance with the residential parent.

Children in this age group need you to be responsible for your own problems and feelings; otherwise they will identify with them and try to rescue you. Sometimes your children's ability to focus completely on you is seductive. If you feel needy, the attention these children give can be hard to resist. But *do* resist, because their focus on you comes at a cost to themselves.

When you are angry with your spouse in front of them, it is important that you be honest about your part in the difficulties between you and the other parent. Also, when you are wrong about something, it is important to apologize.

Adolescents

Adolescents usually become independent from the family by alternating between being mature and being overly dependent. In the mature phase, the adolescent is very critical of his parents; in the dependent phase, he sees them as all-knowing authorities. All of this makes him feel insecure, and he appreciates his family's stability

more than ever. So when his parents separate, he is faced with a difficult task.

Adolescents are at the stage where they are concerned with mo-
rality and right and wrong, so they are likely to side against the
parent they think 'caused' the separation. If parental demands are
too intense, teenagers may pull away from both parents, which
deprives them of the guidance they need to face important life
decisions.

Wallerstein and Kelly's sample (1980) showed that adolescents are
greatly affected by their parents' divorce in the area of mate selec-
tion. Here, the long-lasting 'wounds' show themselves. Adolescents
who experience family disruption can be more cynical about permanence in relationships. They may find it hard to make a commitment
to long-term relationships.

Talk openly with your teenager about love, sex, and commitments.
Be honest about your part in what went wrong between you and his
other parent. Tell him what you have learned and what you would
do differently if you had the chance. Your honesty will allow him to
confide in you, and to make sense of the ending of your relationship.
Tolerate and listen to his fears, his anger, and his feelings about the
separation.

Out of guilt over the divorce, some parents have difficulty listening to their children. They either avoid talking about the divorce, or
become defensive and justify themselves. This cuts off the possibility
of real dialogue and leaves the child alone with his struggles.

THE SPECIAL TASKS OF CHILDREN OF DIVORCE

Wallerstein (1983) noted that children from divorced families must
master an additional set of emotional or psychological tasks.

Children of divorce, like their parents, have to accept the reality of
the divorce. This is why it is important for you to tell them about it.
Wallerstein found that very few parents actually tell their children
they are separating. This results in a double-shock for children. Children also need to know and accept that the separation is final. Only
after they accept that your marriage is over are their reconciliation

fantasies challenged. By telling them you will not be getting back together, you allow them to begin grieving.

Because divorce creates a family crisis, the whole family becomes overinvolved with it. Children become more interested in their parents' lives than in their own. They have to learn to reconnect with their own lives. They have to be able to stand back from your problems and leave them to you. By containing your problems and acting as if you can manage them (even if, at times, you feel like you cannot), you help them reclaim their lives.

You must help your children learn not to blame themselves for your divorce. Like you, they need to endure and manage their feelings of anger and loss. And they have to learn to be realistic about the possibility of permanence in relationships.

Children must also come to terms with the many *losses* that the divorce entails: the loss of living together with both parents, the family home and neighbourhood. Unless children are helped to grieve all their losses, they can feel that they are not lovable. When children grow up in a family that is divorced, they tend to assume that they may themselves divorce when they grow up. So your children need to understand why you and your ex broke up. They need to appreciate that although you are like them, you are also different from them. They will have their own strengths and weaknesses in relationships. They will have the power to decide whether they want to develop a long-term relationship. They need not automatically rule it out. When you openly discuss your marriage and relationships with your children, you create a dialogue that will free them from the fall-out of divorce and separation.

If you want your children to become competent in the world, see yourself as a resource to them. Be open with them about yourself. Tell them what you think and what you feel about yourself, your relationships, and your decisions. Tell them what you would do differently if you had the chance.

When children grow up with the possibility of knowing who they are, they make good choices for themselves. They become competent.

Children's Reactions to Divorce*

Developmental phase	Reactions	How to help
Infancy (0 to 2 years) Needs physical closeness and continuity to one parent.	Children show their generalized insecurity in feeding, toileting, sleeping, and behaviour problems.	Keep their routines and rituals consistent and predictable. Take extra time at leavings. Give extra reassurance, love, and attention. Have the other parent visit often in the home. Make changes gradually. Have visits 1 to 3 hours about 3 times a week.
Between ages 2 and 3 Terrible 'separation' anxiety.	Children experience 'separation anxiety': a generalized fear of loss. They are whiney, more clingy. They want constant contact with the parent they live with most of the time. They cry at leavings and transitions.	Tell your child where the other parent is and why. Ensure that they have frequent short visits with the other parent. Allow for longer visits and eventually a full Saturday. Take extra time at leavings and transitions.
Preschool (3 to 5 years) They use magical thinking.	Children experience separation anxiety: they may be frightened, confused, clingy, whiney, needy.	Tell your child about separation. 'Daddy will live down the street. You'll see him three times a week.'

*These reactions are temporary if well managed.

Children's Reactions to Divorce (*Continued*)

Developmental phase	Reactions	How to help
Fantasy of reconciliation. Fantasy of being central: 'I caused the separation.'	They are afraid of being abandoned, which makes them act in a more babyish manner. They regress to earlier behaviour patterns. They try to get you back together. They feel anxiety and guilt. They have more temper tantrums.	Both of you have to reassure your child: 'We both still love you although we are not together.' Slowly extend the visits into overnights. By 4, the child can manage weekends. Explain that you will not be getting back together. Reassure your child that he did not cause the divorce and cannot get you back together. Handle their tantrums with firm limits, allow for emotional expression of feelings.
Early school age (6 to 8 years) Grief replaces denial. These children feel the anguish the most. They understand about relationships. They understand that the divorce is about the parents' relationship.	Children feel saddened, cry and complain of loss. They are frightened of the future. They can have terrible nightmares. They yearn for the other parent when they are with you. They want their parents to reconcile.	Help them to express feelings of loss and anger. Reassure them about your love. Maintain a clear parenting plan with as much living time with both of you as possible. Both of you must keep in contact with school and activities.

Children's Reactions to Divorce (*Continued*)

Developmental phase	Reactions	How to help
	They may refuse to go to school, they may do less well at school. They may contract unexplained illnesses: stomachache/asthma/headaches. They are afraid of being displaced by the new family and new spouse. They are angry at both parents. They can align with each parent: shifting alliances. They take the role of absent parent with younger siblings.	Encourage their peer relationships and their relationships with significant others (e.g., grandparents). Don't make them feel they have to choose sides. Don't polarize: describe both of you as a mix of good and bad qualities. Provide consistent rules: they should negotiate with each of you about your household rules.
Older school-aged (9 to 12 years) They take a stand about the divorce.	They are shocked, surprised, denying, and disbelieving. They feel intense anger at the parent they think caused the divorce. They may see the parent as selfish to have disrupted their family life. They may blame and reject one parent.	Encourage him to talk with a neutral adult, extended family, or suggest peer counselling. Avoid blaming each other. Support him emotionally. Avoid burdening him with your problems. Maintain the parenting plan regardless of their wishes.

Children's Reactions to Divorce (*Continued*)

Developmental phase	Reactions	How to help
	They are very vulnerable to loyalty conflicts.	Get family counselling prior to a remarriage.
	They are vulnerable to being made an ally to one of you.	Keep the child's life vital: help him with his academic and social life.
	They may complain of frequent, mild somatic problems.	
	They shift between acting very mature and then suddenly very dependent.	
Adolescent (13 to 18 years) Needs to develop separate identity.	They feel ambivalence but are not surprised. They feel pain and anger at loss of family just when they need support. They act mature and then suddenly act very dependent. They are more focused on their peers. They worry about sex and relationships. They worry about the effect of their parents' divorce on their idea of relationships.	Help him become independent, encourage academic achievement, outside interests, and after school activities. At times, encourage active involvement in family, like in structured family meetings. Give lots of emotional support. Maintain limits, rules, discipline, structure. Don't polarize, don't get him caught between you. Encourage contact with both of you. Speak to him honestly about your relationship.

Children's Reactions to Divorce (*Concluded*)

Developmental phase	Reactions	How to help
	They may have difficulty with long-term, romantic relationships because they fear their marriage will fail. They side with the parent they think is at fault.	Encourage sibling and parental support. Maintain family structure. Help adolescents understand that each of you has both good and bad qualities and is responsible for the divorce.

Bonnie E. Robson, MD (1986), *Contemporary Pediatrics*. Adapted.

How Will Your Child Fare?

- Most children resume their normal development two to three years after the separation.
- Your child's adjustment to your divorce depends on how you managed the predivorce conflict between you and your spouse and the quality of parenting you both offered. It also depends on the quality and richness of the parenting plan and the amount of closeness and contact the child has with both of you. It depends greatly on the degree of conflict between you and the other parent and how you manage it. It depends greatly on whether you use your children in that conflict, and whether you go to court.
- Their adjustment depends heavily on your adjustment to your divorce, your financial security, and how you parent after the divorce. It depends on how supportive you are to the child, how much you allow and encourage him to deal with his distress.
- All these variables will interact with your child's temperament, gender, and age at the time of your separation.
- This may seem like an overwhelming list of things that can go wrong; however, you can also see it as a list of things you can make sure will go right.

6. Talking to Your Children about Your Divorce

Parents always find it difficult to talk to their children about painful topics. And talking to them about your divorce is especially hard, because you feel guilty about creating a tough situation for them. As parents, you want to make your children happy, not create problems for them.

Mr P said, 'I had children to make them happy. They did not ask to be born, I chose for them to be, and here I am divorcing their mother. I know it will make them miserable for the short term and maybe longer ... When I realized my divorce was difficult for them, I felt I had lost my innocence as a parent. Here I myself was hurting them.'

Although these sentiments are understandable, you have to let them go. You have good reasons to end your marriage or to accept that it is ending, and although divorce hurts children temporarily, if you handle it well your children will regain their equilibrium.

It is very important to talk to your children about your divorce. The following guidelines will help you to talk to them with competence and sensitivity.

Children Are Very Sensitive to Your Moods, Feelings, and Issues

Because they depend on you for their survival, your children are exquisitely tuned to you. They know, without being told, a lot about what affects you. Children also know what you are not telling them.

But they often misinterpret what they pick up because their minds are not fully developed, so it is best to talk to them straight and clear and at their level. Example: 'I am angry right now but it is not because of you.'

Children Try Hard to Keep You Happy

Children feel secure when their parents are happy. Because they are attuned to you, they know what makes you happy or sad. This makes them experts in promoting your happiness.

When her parents fought, Jennifer did something to distract them. She had a stomachache, threw a tantrum, or suddenly remembered a problem at school. Sometimes she became especially charming.

Children Will Only Discuss with You What You Can Handle

This is related to the above point. Children tend to your feelings. If you feel devastated, angry, or frustrated about your divorce, your children will steer clear of the topic. If you are openly angry with the other parent, your children will give you only negative reports about the other parent because this is what they think you want to hear. Understanding what your children really feel becomes difficult.

Encourage Your Children to Express Their Feelings and Thoughts

Children can handle most things if they are allowed their reactions. When unpleasant things happen to children, they need to protest and have their reactions before they can accept them.

Five-year-old Judy was asked how visits with her father could be improved. She answered, 'The visits would be better if I had a different father.' On further exploration, Judy told us that she was 'tired' of her father and 'needed a new one.' She did not like her father criticizing her mother and not allowing her cat in the house. She also did not like her mother complaining about him. Judy was encouraged to discuss these thoughts with both parents.

TIPS FOR TALKING TO YOUR CHILDREN ABOUT YOUR DIVORCE

Be Emotionally Centred

Because your feelings affect your children, be composed when you speak to them. Be careful and measured when talking to them about something as delicate as your divorce. Don't talk to them about your divorce just after you've had a fight with your ex. They will assume the anger is meant for them. They may feel that you are blaming them for the divorce, or that you want them to be angry at the other parent.

Be Careful Not to Load the Discussion with Feelings That Do Not Belong There

'Dumping' refers to an interaction in which the other person is left with your feelings. Suddenly after talking to you, your child may feel she hates her father, when in fact *you* are the one who just had a nasty exchange with him.

Speak Clearly about the Issue

Say what you want to say in simple language that children can understand. 'Your father and I do not love each other anymore. Your father and I will not be living together in this house anymore. He will be living in an apartment four blocks from here. You will be living with him every week from Thursday until Monday.' When you are clear and direct about your feelings and the reasons for your behaviour your children can understand the reasons for your actions. When children can make sense of the world around them, they become confident.

After You Have Said What You Want, Be Sure the Child Understands

Check it out. You could say, 'Now, what did you hear me say?' If necessary, correct what you said, or how you meant it. Stay with it until you are sure the child understands. In a sensitive area such as divorce, there is plenty of room for misunderstandings.

Ask the Child for His Reactions to What You Said

After you are sure your child heard what you said, ask him how he feels about what he has heard. Asking for feedback promotes intimacy between parents and children. It may take a while for them to be sure you want to hear what they have to say, but if you bring it up, over time, in a gentle way they will eventually speak freely.

Expect Your Child's Point of View to Be Different from Yours

Sometimes divorcing parents feel insecure about their decision to separate and seek support for their point of view. They want it validated. Without meaning to, they discuss their relationship with their spouse with their children in such a way that their children take their side. This may be comforting for parents in the short term, but in the long run it is not. You need to help your children develop their own points of view about the divorce (as well as most other issues). This prepares them for independence. Too many children wait until they are in their 40s to have their own opinion about their parents' relationship.

Feelings and Reactions Keep Changing

If your child tells you he is sad about the divorce, don't assume that the next time you talk to him he will feel exactly the same. It is normal for children's feelings about divorce to fluctuate over time. A child may feel sad about the separation one day, and the next day display anger and irritation about it. Feelings come in layers: after one set of feelings is acknowledged, sometimes a whole different set of feelings emerges. For instance, one day a child may express fears about seeing his mother; the following day, he may have an intense longing to see her.

In the same way, different and sometimes opposite feelings can exist at the same time. For instance, a child can feel angry at his father for leaving, yet at the same time yearn to see him.

Expect Your Child to Be Upset and Then Comfort Him

An upset child of any age needs cuddling, reassurance, and understanding. Hold him while you talk about the separation. Let him cry on your shoulder. Make sure you allow plenty of silences. Sometimes just sitting quietly together is all that is required. Being sad together and being a physical presence can be comforting. When parents create this kind of loving, non-demanding environment that allows children to be themselves, it is called a 'holding environment' (Winnicott, 1965). The parent 'holds' whatever the child is experiencing without trying to influence how the child should feel. Children need this holding because they need comfort and support as they learn to tolerate these painful feelings by themselves.

Try to Ask Open-Ended Questions about Your Children's Feelings

Because children are so suggestible, any indication of what you expect them to feel will colour their response. So, for instance, 'Are you still upset about daddy?' is less helpful than 'How are you feeling now?'

Never Judge Your Children's Feelings

To create a safe place for children to understand and express their feelings, you must avoid judging what they say. When we judge, we do not hear. Moreover, children are very sensitive to being judged: when their feelings are not supported, they easily deny and 'take back' their feelings.

Ask How These Talks Could Be Easier for Him

This implies that you are open to discussing your mistakes and their impact. It also shows that you want to know how you can improve the situation. Talking to children in this way develops their competence. It gives them power in a situation where they had no power and no choice. Your divorce is something that just 'happened' to them. They did nothing to cause it, yet it affects them deeply in every part of their life. When they can talk about it freely, they gain a sense of control.

Do Not Overprotect Your Child

Your child will be stronger for experiencing life, and your separation is part of her life. You cannot protect children from pain and mistakes, yours *or* theirs. Overprotected children do not develop competence; they develop fears. When you feel guilty toward children, you are encouraging them to feel sorry for themselves.

Do Not 'Parentify' Your Child

Children develop the capacity for empathy around the age of 7 or 8, and are very attuned to their parents. It is tempting to use a child's empathy for comfort. According to Wallerstein (1985), children who are used as parental counsellors are 'overburdened'; they are old and wise beyond their years.

Hearing Your Child

As we stated earlier, your children often say what they think you want to hear. If you don't tolerate your ex, your child will tell you negative stories about him. But when allowed to speak their minds, children usually say they love their parents. However, and here is the problem, children will cover up what they really feel or really want to avoid upsetting their parents. A child will say she doesn't want to see her mother, when in fact she does. Or she will say 'I want to live with you' to a father who longs for her to live with him. Sometimes children say so often what their parents want to hear that they become confused about what they really want.

When a child presents the wrong view of himself, we say the child is presenting 'his false self' (Winnicott, 1965) – that is, an untrue image of himself. Winnicott saw the false self as a child's way of adjusting to an environment that cannot accommodate to him. So the child accommodates to the parent. In that process, the child loses touch with his real self. It is better for a child when the parent can listen to him patiently and calmly while he reveals 'his real self.' The real self does not emerge fully formed; rather, it slowly evolves. In this sense, parenting the *real* child is labour intensive.

> - In conflicted situations, children do not necessarily tell the truth.
> - It takes time, skill, and patience to read your children.
> - The investment you make in listening to your child allows him to become his 'real self.'

7. The Parenting Plan

WHAT IS A PARENTING PLAN?

When you separate, the question arises as to how you and your spouse will parent in two separate homes. How will decisions be made? How will the children's education be decided? Where will the children reside? There is bound to be confusion as the two of you wrestle with these questions. Developing a parenting plan helps you handle them. A *parenting plan* is a document that sets out your responsibilities and how you will conduct yourselves with regard to the children so that you can work co-operatively and effectively as separated parents. There is no magic in creating a parenting plan. You can draw it up by yourselves, with or without the help of professionals, such as lawyers and social workers. When you have drawn up your plan, you incorporate it into a formal separation agreement by your lawyers. If you cannot reach agreement voluntarily, an agreement may be imposed upon you by an arbitrator (with your consent to his involvement) or by court order.

Whether your plan is the result of an agreement between you or one that is imposed on you makes a world of difference. If the plan is imposed, one of you will almost certainly be deprived of control over significant aspects of your parenting, this can lead to resentment, animosity, and power struggles. Unfortunately, in high-conflict divorces imposed arrangements are necessary (see Chapter 12). An agreed-upon plan, even one where both of you feel you had to make more compromises than you would have liked, is far better because having authored it, you are more committed to making it work. The negotiating process in itself acknowledges to both of you how you together co-create your parenting role in the new separated family.

Your parenting plan is a work in progress, a document that grows and changes as the children do. Because it sets the foundation for your parenting, it may become the most important document of your family life. If you treat it this way and develop it slowly, carefully, and thoughtfully, it will serve you and your family well. It will reduce conflicts and help avoid headaches. So approach it with care and look upon the time and money you spend on it as a very wise investment.

Money spent on unnecessary litigation is money wasted; money spent on creating a parenting plan is money saved.

When you complete your parenting plan, you feel like very good parents because you have demonstrated to your children that, despite the divorce, they are still number one, and that you will do right by them no matter what. In fact, many parents find that the parenting plan begins to heal the guilt they feel about their children.

'I gotta say this plan was just a piece of paper when we started. I was still so mad at my ex, I just hated having to get together. But after a few weeks talking with her and that great mediator, I started feeling like a whole new thing was happening for us. It was no longer about her and me and who should take the rap. It was about Christine, our 5-year-old, and that she needed to come through this without a lot of damage. My ex and I didn't care if we damaged each other, but we both cared about not damaging Christine. And you know what? We got so focused on this task that one day I looked up, and I saw in my ex the very thoughtful person I had married long, long ago. She is still that thoughtful person, when it came to Christine, and was I glad to see that!'

Does a Parenting Plan Mean Joint Custody?

No. A parenting plan sets out the decision-making and residential arrangements for the separating family. It can result in any kind of living arrangements, from a child living almost half-time with each parent to a child living primarily with one parent and living with the other parent on alternate weekends. The arrangement possibilities are limited only by imagination and practical considerations. The plan may also set down that one parent has the final say about decisions regarding education, health, and so on, or it may make allowances for you to use a meditor or an arbitrator to settle disputes.

When Should a Parenting Plan Be Made?

It is best to draw up your parenting plan before you separate. Then, when you talk to your children (hopefully together) about your intention to separate, you will have a concrete plan to show them. The existence of the plan will allay their fears of losing either of you. Drawing up your parenting plan as early as possible gets you off to a good start and may save you months and years of useless argument and futile litigation. The only drawback to doing your plan early is that you and your spouse may still be too angry with each other to negotiate well together. You may still be unable to control the urge to place blame, or to fight to gain some relief from the pain.

Children Love to See the Parenting Plan

A parenting plan creates a real sense of security for children. They usually experience it as the calm in the storm of the divorce. They are reassured when they see how their parents have planned ahead, how every detail of their lives has been anticipated. They feel profoundly comforted to know that *their parents are divorcing each other, not divorcing them.*

'I couldn't believe it,' said 11-year old Tommy. 'With all the fighting and the screaming, I was sure I'd end up with nothing and no one. I felt I would never see one of my parents, like Tammy down the street, who never sees her father. And no soccer, no hockey, no money. I had nightmares about where we'd be living and what school I'd have to go to. And then just when I felt

the worst ever, I saw their parenting plan — well, really, I didn't see it, but they both told me about it. Wow! Everything was there, even plans for when I go to camp for the next five years. What really blew my mind was that I would be living with both of them. It was all written down, so you knew it was going to work out.'

The Problem with Words

The more co-operative 'human' language of parenting plans is slowly replacing the rigid terminology of litigation. 'Custody' and 'access' are legalistic terms that remind you of prison and probation rather than family life. They are loaded words that reinforce parents' fears of losing their children. Implicit in these words is the idea that the victorious parent 'gets' custody or possession of the children – as if children were chattels or objects to be owned. They fail to convey the essentially creative activity of two parents trying to encompass their children's needs within a two-unit family structure.

A parenting plan that outlines parental responsibilities transforms the win/lose of the custody battle into the peaceful win/win feeling of shared responsibilities. You fight for custody and access rights, but do you fight for shared parental responsibilities?

Having said that, the term 'sole custody' in the sense of sole decision-making, is to be used when one parent must assume responsibility for a child who is at risk from the behaviours of the other parent. This risk can arise for a variety of reasons, including a history of family violence, child abuse, or neglect, or the threat of kidnapping.

Do Parenting Plans Increase Your Co-operation?

Yes. The careful detailing of parental responsibilities paves the way to parental co-operation. When responsibilities are carefully spelled out, each parent feels more secure, with a defined role to play in the child's life. That role becomes enshrined in law. Each plan provides for what to do when parents disagree by building in a mechanism for dispute resolution. All of this encourages co-operation and reduces insecurity.

ISSUES TO ADDRESS IN PARENTING PLANS

Parenting plans usually address three areas: parenting guidelines, decision making, living arrangements.

Parenting Guidelines

These are guidelines for parental behaviour. Often, parenting plans start with parents putting words to a behavioural code that they both agree on: 'From now on, this is how we will behave ...' Parents usually see the benefits of establishing such guidelines because good behaviour goes a long way toward generating good will and a sense of a new beginning.

One father felt that creating guidelines removed his sense of anxiety at transfers. When picking up Samantha, he just never knew what to expect from her mother. 'Will she? Won't she? Get mad, give me the cold shoulder, yell, criticize, or alienate?' With the guidelines in place, he assumed they would both behave. 'The best part is that every time we treat each other courteously is like money in the bank. It's like something to draw on. Each good time seems to cancel out some of the bad stuff we did to each other before and during the separation. I figure in two years we'll be just about at par.'

The guidelines require you to respect each other as parents even though you may be angry and disappointed in each other as spouses. Even if only one parent respects the other as a parent, the conflict between them decreases.

Content of the Guidelines

You may want to include the following items in your guidelines:

1. We will keep our conflict away from the children.
2. We will not denigrate each other in front of the children.
3. We will keep adult matters such as legal and financial issues firmly between us and away from the children.

4. We will not burden our children with our feelings of sadness and loneliness related to the break-up.
5. We will not ask our children to choose between us. Not by a look, a shrug of the shoulders, or a careless word. We will encourage them to love us both.

Decision Making

Decision making is the nuts and bolts of parenting. It is important for you and the children to know who makes what decisions. A parenting plan clarifies the decision-making process for everyone.

Day-to-Day Decisions

Each of you is in charge of what happens in your own home, and this should be set out in the plan. Problems arise when you assume you should control day-to-day decisions made in the other home. Day-to-day issues are to be decided by the parent who is with the children at the time. These decisions include those pertaining to nutrition, discipline, babysitting, emergency medical issues, and the children's extracurricular activities during their time with you.

Dispute Resolution Clause

Important issues not anticipated in the plan sometimes arise after the plan is in place. For instance, what to do when you differ on which school Bobby should attend, or when you differ on whether he should get dental braces. There are several ways to deal with these kinds of disagreements. One parent might be placed in charge of certain issues, such as education, or you might agree to accept the opinion of a professional with expertise in the specific area in which you disagree. For instance, some parents agree to abide by the child's doctor's opinion in medical matters. Many plans include a provision for a 'mediator/arbitrator' to resolve differences. This proviso guarantees that if decisions cannot be reached through mediation, you will agree to accept the recommendations of the mediator/arbitrator.

The difference between a mediator and an arbitrator is that a mediator helps the two of you work through a problem to an agreement; whereas an arbitrator, after considering each of your positions, makes a decision to which you will both adhere. In some plans, the parents agree that one professional can wear both the hats of a mediator and arbitrator.

When One Parent Wants to Move

Every parenting plan sets out procedures to follow in the event that one of you wants to move to a distant town or city. For example, what should be done if one of you has been offered a job in another city two hundred miles away and wants to move with the children? Problems of relocation are very challenging to address; and mediation, arbitration, or the courts will focus on the best solution for the children.

Annual Reviews of the Parenting Plan

Because children grow and circumstances change, many plans include provisions for an annual review where the parents meet, with or without a mediator, to review the children's progress and consider any required changes.

Living Arrangements

Deciding on the right living arrangements for your children is a creative process that takes many factors into consideration. Some of these factors are the ages and temperaments of the children, their attachment to each of you, how the children were cared for before the divorce, your respective work schedules, your wishes, and your parenting abilities. The children may appreciate your listening to their ideas about the kind of parenting plan they want. However, it is important to reassure them that you will make the final decisions about the schedule.

The living arrangements should not be predetermined by assumptions. For instance, some parents assume that 'access' always means every second weekend and one overnight each week. Others assume that the children should spend equal time in each house. These formulaic arrangements disregard your children's particular needs and restrict you in determining what is best for your family.

Often, it is difficult to agree on living arrangements when one of you wants more time with the children than your children's needs justify. When this happens a mediator will help you experiment by putting in place temporary arrangements that allow you to assess their effects on the children. The knowledge you gain can help you to fine-tune the best plan for them.

It is better for children if you both live in the same neighbourhood, or at least not too far from each other. This allows them the continuity of friends and community facilities. Children appreciate these continuities when their families are coming apart.

Age Considerations

When deciding on your living arrangements, refer to the following guidelines about what children of different ages need.

0–3 Years

Infants need closeness and continuity with one parent. They also need predictability and familiarity. This means that an infant should live primarily in one home, with the other parent visiting the child for regular, frequent, and short visits, preferably in the primary home. We recommend a minimum of three visits per week, each visit lasting from one to three hours. When the child is a toddler, she can manage longer times and the visits can be expanded to a full day. Eventually the child will be ready for overnights with the other parent. Children who are just starting overnights feel reassured when accompanied by older siblings.

There is controversy about overnights, with some experts (Hodges, 1986) suggesting that a child cannot handle overnights until she is at least 3; others (Adler, 1988) believe that a child who has been accustomed to several visits every week since birth is able to handle overnights by 6 months. Children who can manage overnight visits at this early age are children who are temperamentally easy-going and securely attached to both parents, and who have not been exposed to parental conflict. Children in day care cannot handle overnights at such an early age because of their reduced time with the primary residential parent. When in doubt, the safest guideline is to wait until your child is 3 years old before instituting overnight visits.

3–6 Years

The child's times with the other parent should be predictable, regular, and frequent. The ideal is at least two visits a week, with no more than a week between visits. After the age of 3, children can extend the one overnight so that by 4 years of age, they are ready for a full weekend. Some experts (Adler, 1988) suggest that a mature, flexible, well-attached child of 3 can manage three overnights; however, children generally find three overnights a week taxing, and we do not recommend it.

6–12 Years

Children over 6 can manage a wider variety of arrangements. Children who see their parents several times a week are the most content, as long as there is low conflict between the parents. Possible arrangements for children of this age group include the following:

A. Sharing time equally by:
- Alternating weeks, with or without a midweek overnight.
- Dividing each week in half, with one parent having the child every Monday and Tuesday, the other parent having the child every Wednesday and Thursday, and the weekends being alternated.
B. Having one primary residence with:
- Alternating weekends beginning on Thursday or Friday, and ending on Sunday evening or Monday morning, with a midweek dinner or overnight.
- Alternating weekends, with dinner every Wednesday evening. Once every month, the weekend parent has the child for a Monday to Friday period.

Sometimes transporting the child to and from school and activities increases the child's contact with a parent. Phone calls reassure the child about his parent's availability.

Teenagers

Parenting plans need to allow for the fact that teenagers have lives of their own. They want to be with their friends, attend their own activities, and be in charge of their time. Time with their parents is not always their first priority. Sometimes they prefer a plan that sets out a primary home, with opportunities for dinners and outings with the other parent. If both parents live in the same neighbourhood, teenagers may enjoy alternating weekends or alternating two-week schedules between the two homes. If your teenager has his own phone number, remind him to set the call-forward so that his friends can find him when he switches homes.

A Word about Holidays

Holidays allow for more flexibility than the regular schedule. Three-year-olds who are used to time away from their primary parent might be able to handle three or four days away from him or her. Make sure you give them all the separation aids they need: photos, special comfort toys and cuddles, telephone contact, audiotapes of their favourite lullabies sung by the primary parent, and so on. Children older than 4 can usually manage week-long holidays. Seven-year-olds can manage two-week holidays. Older children and teens may want to spend most of the holidays with the other parent.

Special Issues

• If you and your spouse cannot treat each other civilly at children's transfers, you must reduce the child's experience of the conflict between you. You could arrange transfers at neutral locations such as school, or day care, or a grandparents' home. Alternatively, you might establish a plan that contains fewer transitions and longer visits.

- Children often benefit from time alone with each parent.
- Children older than 7 often need more time with the parent of the same gender. Sometimes older children may ask to live with the parent of the same gender. This does not necessarily mean they have a problem with the other parent.

8. Getting to Your Parenting Plan

There are many processes available to help you achieve your parenting plan. The six basic processes are (1) deciding by yourselves; (2) using lawyers to negotiate for you; (3) mediation; (4) mediation with premediation counselling; (5) arbitration; and (6) court, possibly with the assistance of a clinical assessment or the Office of the Children's Lawyer.

1. Deciding Together

In this process, you and your spouse attend a series of meetings to settle on your parenting plan. This option allows you complete control over decision making, but it will only work if you and your spouse have some trust in each other and are able to negotiate calmly together. If this process is to work well, you and your spouse must both be assertive, there can be no serious power imbalance between you, and both of you must be knowledgeable about the implications of your decisions. For example, you must both understand that if conflict arises in the future, the parent who lives with the children has a legal advantage. For this reason, it is important that you have your plan reviewed by a lawyer before it is finalized.

2. Using Lawyers to Negotiate for You

Hiring a lawyer does not necessarily mean you will go to court. It just means that you want to create a parenting plan but do not want to negotiate face to face. Your lawyers will do that for you as well as protect your respective legal rights. The disadvantage of hiring lawyers is that you place your decision making in their hands, and lawyers are trained in the 'adversarial' method. Consequently, the focus may shift from *problem-solving* about what's best for your children to *competing for the most time with the children* (or for the title of 'sole custody'). An enlightened family lawyer will try to negotiate from the perspective of the children's best interests, but you must keep in mind that the legal system is still adversarial in nature. Remember that your lawyer's role is to give you legal advice and negotiate for *you*, but you always have the final say. When all the negotiations are over, you and the other parent will still have to carry on as a parental team.

3. Mediation

In this process, you and your spouse meet together with a neutral third party who helps you develop your plan. Anyone – for example, a trusted friend, a relative or a therapist – can act as a mediator. But because the development of a parenting plan can be a complicated task, we recommend that you hire a professional mediator who specializes in creating parenting plans.

The process of mediation requires you to put aside your spousal conflict and follow certain rules of communication and procedure. This does not mean that you do not express conflicts about parenting issues. Of course you do. You use mediation *because* you are in conflict, *but you express your conflict in order to resolve it*, not escalate it. A mediator will help you put aside your difficulties with each other, leave the past behind, and concentrate on your children's needs.

Research (Kelly, 1993) indicates that when parents use mediation, they experience less conflict and more co-operation. Successful mediation reduces animosities and helps parents achieve an emotional divorce from each other, which is just a few steps away from creating a good divorce for the children.

If you have been physically abused by your spouse and are too intimidated to speak your mind in the presence of your ex-partner, it is absolutely crucial that you inform your mediator of this fact. Mediation under these circumstances may not be appropriate. If after consultation the decision is made to proceed, the mediator *will take care to correct the imbalance of power and ensure safety.*

Attitudes for Successful Mediation

- Deal with the past spousal relationship on your own, not with the other parent.
- Forgive both yourself and your ex-spouse.
- See yourselves as partners in the business of rearing children.
- Be future oriented.
- Focus on the children.

Mediation gives you control of the process and the outcome. It involves you in a respectful, unifying process that is supportive of both of you and may heal some of the wounds of your divorce. It allows you to arrive at an arrangement tailored to your family's particular needs.

4. Mediation with Premediation Counselling

Mediation with premediation counselling is a good option for you and your spouse if you want to mediate but find that you are too angry or hurt to even imagine being in the same room, let alone being able to act civilly or co-operatively.

Premediation counselling helps you explore your anger and hurt with your spouse in a safe and private space. Often, parents ignore or minimize their contributions to their fighting and truly believe that they are not fighting, even though it is clear to those around them that they are fully engaged in the conflict.

We often do not know ourselves as well as we think we do. In particular, we do not know what is happening in our unconscious. Thus we must *be aware and beware.* We can all remember times when we acted on impulses we did not fully understand. For instance, have you ever suddenly spent $200 on an outfit you did not really need only later to realize that you bought the outfit because you were anxious about an upcoming social occasion? You hoped that the new outfit would make you feel more secure. In a situation like this, the consequences of being out of touch with your feelings are small: at worst, you have an extra outfit. But being out of touch with your feelings, and inadvertently escalating problems in parent child arrangements, can have huge consequences. It can undermine your attempts at mediation, push you to litigate unnecessarily, and throw your life into turmoil for years and years with the end result that your family will never be the same again.

Premediation counselling helps each of you become aware of how you are behaving with the other, and of the deeper feelings associated with your behaviours. You begin to understand yourselves and to appreciate which of your behaviours are contributing to the conflicts. Achieving a certain level of self-understanding allows you to change your contribution to the conflict. If at least one of you achieves this self-management, the conflicts lessen. It usually takes two to create a fight. Realize your contribution to the conflict.

Jennifer withheld overnight access because she was sure it would overtax her 3-year-old daughter, Julie. When her ex became angry, she assumed he was just being difficult as usual. She talked to a friend who told her that children as young as 3 are able to manage overnights if the parents cooperate. Jennifer was surprised but she still did not let Julie go. She wondered about this information, which she brought to the first premediation counselling session. With the help of the counselling, she came to realize that she needed Julie in the house for her own comfort. She was delighted when Julie came into her bed at night; Julie's presence comforted her for the loss of her husband. With this new understanding she agreed to Julie's going to her father's for the night. It wasn't easy. On the first overnight, she became very upset. She called her friend and cried about missing Julie. To her friend, she confided how much she missed the comfort of sleeping with her husband. She divulged how much she missed their closeness and she wept for the loss of those times. In the counselling she discussed how hard it was to accept her husband's leaving. She was able to better understand why she had opposed Julie's overnights.

Premediation counselling helps you accept and tolerate the limitations of your situation.

Mr R. felt that his wife was not being a good mother to their 6-year-old child. He felt she should spend more time with her, work less, and not leave her with relatives. He was nudged into realizing that he was expecting more than she was able to give and more than their child actually needed. He was encouraged to mourn that he had no control over what went on in his ex's home.

Therapy is a more intense form of counselling that tries to help you track down the source of negative behaviour patterns. Therapy helps clarify so called 'neurotic' problems, that is, problems that arise from confusions between your current life and your childhood. It is surprising how many parents, in fighting each other, are fighting earlier battles. At Toronto's 'For Kids' Sake,' we often find that parents who cannot resolve their conflicts have histories of childhood abuse and neglect, parental divorce, dislocation, and abandonment. Once they begin to acknowledge such tragedies, they are more able to recognize certain patterns in their behaviour. These patterns may have helped them cope with difficulties in the distant past, but are now, perhaps, causing or maintaining problems between them and their ex-partners.

5. Arbitration

For couples who try to mediate but cannot arrive at an agreement, arbitration may be the answer. In this process, the parents and their lawyers select an arbitrator – a professional with knowledge and expertise in the area of their dispute. The arbitrator will consider their respective positions and make a decision as to the best course of action. The parents must adhere to the arbitrator's decision.

6. The Courts

The last resort in all conflicts is submitting the dispute to a judge. Although lawyers and clients often threaten to take this step, they rarely do. Most cases are resolved through ongoing mediative efforts or negotiations between lawyers as the case proceeds through the court system. However, when negotiations are deadlocked and the parents cannot agree on arbitration, either parent may choose to have his/her day in court. The other parent must put in an appearance. The judge renders a decision, to which the parents must abide.

The disadvantage of this option is that courts cannot tailor a plan to suit your family's particular needs. The court is at arm's length and cannot have intimate knowledge of your family's needs. Courts usually create plans that are 'one size fits all.' We discuss this in greater detail in Chapter 12.

When the court is asked to order a plan for the children, it often appoints a social worker, psychologist, or psychiatrist to assess the situation and provide recommendations as to what would be best. During such an assessment, the parents often come to an agreement and settle on a parenting plan. (This is discussed in greater detail in Chapter 12.)

If you are concerned that your children's needs are being jeopardized, you can request the court to involve a children's lawyer to protect the interests of your children. In Ontario, this function is carried out by the government's Office of the Children's Lawyer. This office will provide a lawyer, who will meet with the children and then represent them in court. If the children's lawyer has clinical concerns, such as relating to emotional abuse or parental alienation, he can recommend the services of a social worker attached to the Office of the Children's Lawyer.

Summary

Parenting plans help you deal with problems that seem overwhelming at the point of separation. In that very difficult time when emotions run high, and there is confusion about how to divide up the responsibilities for the children, you can each reclaim a sense of control by co-creating a parenting plan. Although living together is no longer possible, parenting together must continue. A parenting plan makes that happen in a respectful and co-operative way. As you share your needs, your fears, and your concerns about the children, you are reassured that there is a way to keep parenting together.

Part II
Managing Conflict by Getting Informed

9. The High-Conflict Divorce

For between 15 and 25 per cent of the divorcing couples, arriving at a parenting plan through mediation or counselling is simply not possible. These parents seem unable to overcome their hostility and conflict. In this chapter, we discuss why certain parents fight; in the next, we discuss how children react to these fights. Later still, we will talk about the dynamics of traditional parenting arrangements, whether chosen or imposed.

UNDERSTANDING PARENTAL CONFLICT: WHY SOME COUPLES CONTINUE TO FIGHT

Johnston and Campbell (1988), in California, studied a group of parents who continued to fight two to ten years after separating. These parents felt they had to fight each other and take each other to court. Sometimes, for instance, these parents were convinced the other parent posed a threat to the well-being of the children, and they wanted the children's access stopped or restricted. When these allegations were carefully and professionally assessed, the children were not found to be at risk. But these parents did not believe it. Even after clear clinical feedback, they stuck to their original allegations and resumed fighting. At other times they fought over schedules, the differing versions of their history, or over who was to blame. Nothing could stop their fighting. It seemed, to these researchers that these parents *fought for the sake of fighting*.

However absurd these situations look, on closer examination it seems that for some parents fighting serves a useful purpose. Fighting helps certain parents to ward off the pain of grieving. When the parents fight, neither feels pain nor sadness. Both feel mad, but not sad. It is as though the fighting distracts them from pain. Intrigued, the researchers set out to explore what causes parents to take this direction. What situations lead to this type of fighting? What makes some parents, who obviously love their children, draw those children into terrible wars? What causes one parent to set the children up against the other parent? And why do some of these wars go on forever?

The answers to these questions are rooted in the psychology of the situation at hand. The following are some of the factors in play:

- A sense of failure about the break-up of the marriage.
- An emotionally traumatic separation.
- A destructive marriage.
- Concerns about the other parent's parenting.
- The parents' self-esteem.
- Seeing the other parent as all bad.
- The parents' overattachment to the children.
- A parent's own childhood trauma, which influences present circumstances.
- The legal system and certain facets of the mental health system, which promote the fighting.

As you read through the reasons why parents fight, you may see some parts of yourself or of your situation. This is to be expected: *all* divorces contain some of these dynamics. It is a high-conflict divorce when these dynamics are extreme, or when you cannot settle things.

If when you read you see only your ex-partner's problems but not your own, beware. *It is rare that only one parent is the problem.* It happens, but it is not common. So if you only see your ex in the following, look again and ask yourself, *'If I had a part in this, what would it be?'*

A Sense of Failure about the Break-up of the Relationship

Some couples feel a crushing sense of failure when their relationship is over. Feeling like this is understandable because although there is not much of a stigma left to divorce, in a subtle way our society still blames couples when they end their relationship. This is unfortunate. Relationships are hard enough to end without couples feeling blamed or that they failed.

When you are criticized, do not take it personally, because only you know what happened between you and your ex. Some couples feel such a sense of personal failure about their divorce that they blame each other. Sometimes a parent goes to court to prove that the other parent is the one at fault; such parents are litigating to 'get' the 'guilty' party. Some parents seek out clinical assessments that will prove them to be 'the good guys' and the other, 'the bad ones.' This is using mental health services to punish your partner. It is a sign of maturity for you to forgive yourself and the other parent for whatever mistakes were made.

Jack took Susan to court because he thought her an unfit mother. Although he was initially convincing, the clinical assessment did not find Susan unfit. During the interviews, he confided that he was mortified about the ending of his marriage. He had expected his marriage to be long-term, like his parents' thirty-year marriage. He felt ashamed and inadequate about his inability to manage relationships. He was sure there were unforgivable things about him that contributed to the marriage breakdown. He was convinced that everyone could see these failings, and he felt anxious about his future.

An Emotionally Traumatic Separation

Sometimes you keep fighting because you were traumatized by the way you separated. The very shock of a highly charged separation makes it hard for you to move on. You feel stuck in anger and protest.

Joe came home to an empty house; his wife and 5-year-old son were gone. He discovered that his wife had gone to a women's shelter, even though there had been no abuse in their relationship. He felt shocked and humiliated. He worried that people might think he had been abusive. He took his wife to court to prove to her, to himself, and to everyone else that he was 'no wife abuser.'

When your partner leaves you in an abrupt and terrible way, you are too mad to grieve. You feel you *have* to fight in order to regain a sense of control and reclaim your self-worth. Going to court can seem like a good way to get revenge. If the judge awards you custody, you will feel victorious. It will prove you were right, and maybe then it will not hurt as much. Sadly, in family matters, courts rarely satisfy this need. And it certainly does not build a good working relationship between you. It only increases your conflict: whoever loses often hires another lawyer and returns to court. The best way to heal the wounds is to face the hurt. This will limit the damage.

A Destructive Marriage

Sometimes fighting is how you relate to each other. A highly combative marriage often carries its antagonisms over into the divorce. Bad marriages seem to be as hard to leave as bad childhoods. Abuse in marriage, like humiliation in childhood, erodes your self-confidence. And you need a lot of self-confidence to make a clean break of your marriage. Leaving a bad situation takes self-respect, and it is hard to feel any self-respect when you are in a bad relationship. Marriages in which there is spousal abuse are the most difficult to leave. When you finally leave a relationship in which you have been abused, you are often left worrying whether your partner is now abusing the children.

During her marriage, Alice had been hit by her husband. After her divorce, she was terrified whenever her son visited his father. She was afraid he too was being physically abused. She took her ex-husband to court to stop her son's access to his father. The clinical assessment revealed that her ex-husband had not abused his son, not during or after the marriage. Alice needed to have her husband acknowledge and express regret for his abuse of her. Only then was she able to work through her fears with a clinician and agree to supervised access.

If you are a parent who has physically abused your spouse, you often cannot appreciate the effect of your behaviour. You don't understand your ex's fear of you, nor do you understand why your children are frightened too. You do not understand that when children witness spousal abuse, they become frightened. You feel that your wife is exaggerating incidents that were mutual shoving or hitting. You feel that you were provoked, and that you were usually defending yourself from her anger. You get angry when your wife and children refuse contact.

Because Mr B's own father hit his mother, he did not see his violence as a problem. He saw violence as the way men deal with women's provocations. When his wife drew a line by leaving him and then restricting his time with his son, he saw her as withholding access out of revenge. His children, however, had their own fears of him. When they refused to get into the car, he became loud, insistent, and bullying. This reinforced the children's and their mother's fear of him.

Methods of handling these complex situations are discussed in Chapter 13.

Concerns about the Other Parent's Parenting

When one parent is worried that the other parent is abusing or neglecting a child, it makes it difficult for them to agree on post-separation arrangements. Sometimes parents have these concerns because they have seen the other parent abuse or neglect the child. These are valid child welfare concerns, which are understandably frightening. Valid parenting concerns must be addressed and settled, with or without court (see Chapters 12 and 13).

But at other times, parents are afraid the other parent is hurting the children and have no evidence or experience to justify their fears. When you are caught in an intense conflict with your ex and worry about your children being hurt, you often *cannot tell* whether your concerns are valid or whether they come from fears. Your fears are so compelling that you are sure they are valid, and yet they may not be. Because of what you have been through, you cannot be sure that your reality check is secure. You have experienced so much destructiveness in the relationship that you only imagine the worst about the other parent's relationship with the child. This can cause you to over-worry and to think that the other parent is being abusive or neglectful, when he is not. Or you can under-worry and, out of fear of escalating the conflict, minimize valid child welfare concerns. You can think the other parent is an acceptable risk parent, when she is not.

For all these reasons, when you have child welfare concerns it is best to inform child welfare agencies and then address them through a clinical assessment. That way, concerns and allegations can be dealt with in a straightforward manner. The assessment process is discussed in detail in Chapter 12.

Also, parents in a fight – especially a litigated one – often use parenting concerns to build a case to restrict or exclude access.

Sonia wondered if her husband John, who was a recovered alcoholic, was leaving their 4-year-old daughter in the care of his relatives. She knew they could not take care of her because they were heavy drinkers. She raised her worries with the clinician during the assessment. While she was aware of positive reports from John's addictions counsellor, employer, and family doctor, she still worried about John's judgment. She met with John and his relatives to discuss her concerns. They agreed that for a few months she could 'drop in' unexpectedly on weekend visits to evaluate John's supervision of the child.

During another assessment, it became clear that 3-year-old Ryan was being left alone while his mother visited friends in the same apartment complex. His father, Jeff, had suspected this was happening, but was afraid that raising these concerns would increase his ex-wife's anger with him. He worried she would restrict his contact with his son. As it turned out, Ryan needed more time with his father.

The Parents' Self-Esteem

Sometimes you fight because you cannot get along without each other. You have come to need each other's support to feel good about yourselves. You feel inadequate in yourself and look to your partner to keep you together. Some of this happens in all relationships: we all look to our partners to support us. But in the situations we are discussing it is more than the usual support: you *need* your partner to *complete* your sense of yourself. When your relationship comes apart, one or both of you feels terribly vulnerable and insecure. At times you feel like you are disintegrating, or falling apart inside. This is called 'separation anxiety' (see Chapter 3), and it is one of the most painful states to endure. Sometimes to get away from it, you find yourself litigating. Fighting makes you feel strong again.

Also, if you are scared to be alone and feel strongly rejected when your relationship ends, litigating keeps you close to your partner. It lets you continue to see your ex in court every so often. If you feel like this, you need special supports when you separate.

Helen took Richard to court because she felt he was not involved enough with the children. She called him almost every day with some complaint or other. She wanted the car or stove fixed, and bawled him out for his lateness or ill treatment of one of their girls. She did not realize how these calls kept her involved with Richard. She was taken aback when Richard complained that she was 'harassing' him. Helen learned that she was avoiding facing the loss of her marriage by staying connected to Richard. Only after making new friends was she able to begin mourning her loss and stop calling Richard.

Seeing the Other Parent as All Bad

Sometimes you fight because you see each other as worse than you are. You focus on the 'terrible things' about each other. You 'demonize' each other. Remembering insults, abuses, and outrages becomes an obsession. If you cannot see anything good in the other parent, you can go to court, but it will not necessarily resolve the problem of how you see him. Also, when you have hurt each other, you sometimes think your whole relationship was negative. You do what Johnston and Campbell (1988) call 'rewriting the story.' You remember things being worse than they were, and that makes you fight more.

If you keep thinking only about your spouse's negative qualities, you must ask yourself why. At one time you were probably in love. You have to remember some of the good times you shared. You must 'rehumanize' your partner. This may make you sad, because it will start your grieving. Although grieving is painful, it will move you out of your anger. Demonizing keeps you stuck in anger.

The Parents' Overattachment to the Children

Sometimes you fight and make all sorts of allegations against each other, not because there is a parent–child problem, but because although you are not aware of it, you want the child to be with you all the time. This makes you want to exclude the other parent. You cannot stand being without the child, even for a weekend. Your own sense of security seems tied to being with your child. You feel very anxious when the child is out of your sight and with the other parent.

When you feel anxious when your child is at the other parent's home, you think it means that your child is not okay there. But your anxiety is really about you being without the child. This is a sign that you are overinvolved with your child, as if you and your child were one person.

A child caught in an overinvolved relationship like this feels burdened. An overly close parent–child bond can develop into a 'parental alienation syndrome,' where the overly close parent turns the child against the other parent. We discuss this in Chapter 10.

George loved his 5-year-old son Jimmy 'to bits.' He hovered over him and took him to and from school, Cubs, and swimming. He loved being with Jimmy. He did not like Jimmy going to his mother's every second weekend and complained about her care of him. Jimmy told his dad that his mother's meals were not as good as his. George became worried that Jimmy's mother was not feeding him enough. When Jimmy cried after coming home, George worried that Jimmy was being mistreated at his mother's. He remembered difficult experiences he'd had with his ex. Jimmy began to notice that complaining about his mother got him immediate attention from his father. One day, Jimmy said 'I hate her' when his mother was twenty minutes late.

George took immediate action, thinking that Jimmy was being mistreated by his mother.

In a high-conflict divorce, mistrust and poor communication allow you to overlook your own problems and focus only on difficulties with the other parent. When you do this, you often deny your own contribution to the problem. When both parents do this, it becomes very difficult for them to see who 'owns' the problem. In the above family, George's overattachment to Jimmy resulted in him seeing neglect where it did not exist.

A Parent's Own Childhood Trauma Which Influences Present Circumstances

If you have experienced earlier loss and abuse, you are probably carrying some unresolved pain that is preventing you from feeling your current losses. This can push you toward litigation as a means to ward off past and current pain. You are *fighting* instead of grieving.

In the 'For Kid's Sake' program, parents are offered help to experience their earlier losses. They are then better able to deal with their current problems.

Sandra and Ted fought like cats and dogs. They could not be married or divorced. Sandra left Ted when the elder of their two boys was 5, and five years later they were still in and out of court. Instead of focusing on their children's distress, they litigated and blamed each other relentlessly. In the group it became clear that Sandra and Ted had been unable to grieve earlier losses. Sandra's mother had left her when she was five, and she had been unable to commit herself to relationships. She found herself 'coming and going' in her children's lives. Ted's mother had died and left his father to raise him and his brother. Remembering how much, as a boy, he had missed his mother, Ted could not tolerate his wife leaving him and their sons. His anger with his wife was loaded with the anger he never expressed about his mother's death. To let his wife go, Ted first had to grieve the death of his mother. To reconnect to her children, Sandra first had to face her mother's abandonment of her.

'The Blaming Hamster'

During our marriage we were like two hamsters on a wheel. We ran furiously, going nowhere, hating our lives and unable to change.

I couldn't change because he wouldn't. So it was his fault. I was trying and he wasn't. It could not be my fault, he was to blame.

Eventually, I couldn't stand it. I jumped off the wheel, left the cage, and took my sons with me. There on the outside I discovered another wheel. Beside it was one for him. We took up residence on our respective wheels. The boys had to dance on the top of the wheels while we continued our war with each other. Although I never returned to the marriage, I lived out a slightly altered version of it. That too was his fault. I could not get on with my life because of him. He would do something. I would latch onto it, using his actions to justify my own.

It took years of this craziness before I saw what it was doing to us. For years I watched my sons bounce back and forth, trying to please us, and paying such a price. One day, way too late, I admitted that I, as well as their father, was damaging them. I realized I could change only myself. I could not change him. Then, to my horror, I noticed that our sons had spun out of control. While we were fighting, they had slowly become delinquent, and we had not even noticed.

Jennifer's metaphor, of the hamster caught on the treadmill, captures the experience of parents caught in these conflicts. Both parents feel they have no choice, that they are forced by the other parent's behaviour to fight. The one fighting causes the other to fight, and there is no way out.

- The only way out is to invest in what you can control: yourself and your behaviour.
- Fighting postpones grieving and increases your problems.
- Focus on what you can change, even if you feel that your ex causes most of the problems.
- The only one you can control is yourself.

The Legal System and Certain Facets of the Mental Health Systems Which Promote the Fighting

The legal system escalates your conflicts. The adversarial nature of that system polarizes problems. A win/lose, right/wrong approach may work in criminal issues, but in family matters a win/win approach is needed. Some lawyers are more hard-nosed than the parents they represent.

In the mental health system, some clinical assessments pit parents against each other by choosing 'the better parent' instead of focusing on how to involve both with their children. Sometimes in high-conflict situations, one parent takes a child for therapy to a setting where only one parent is seen. This is often a poor approach, because the clinician sees only half of the picture, which can exacerbate problems.

Stay in charge of the systems you consult, and whose services you employ. They are there to serve you, not to rule you. Always inquire about their philosophy and orientation. Many family court lawyers and judges are trained in mediation and take the child's interests as their starting point. Avoid legal intervention if possible; if you must use it, be absolutely sure it is focusing on the child. Courts should be used to ensure the *child's* rights, not the parents' rights.

10. The Impact of Conflict on Children and Parental Alienation Syndrome

How Parents Use Their Children in the Fight

When parents quarrel for years, they are placing their children in a war zone. Absorbed by the fighting, they neglect and misinterpret the needs of their children. When parents are in a fight, they organize themselves to win – sometimes at any cost. In that struggle, they often enlist their children's support, thereby turning them against the other parent. They encourage the children to take sides, to love one and not the other. They use them as pawns, as trophies, as spies and informants. The children are seen as something to fight over, as prizes to win to prove that one parent is better than the other. When the children return from the other parent's home, they are cross-examined about the details of that parent's life. Some parents use their children as mediators on a 'peacekeeping' mission to their ex. Parents who act in these ways are, without meaning to, emotionally abusing their children.

A 17-year-old survivor of a bitter, litigated divorce: 'She hates my father, but she always wants to know everything about him. I hate coming home. She's there waiting for me with the twenty questions. "So ...?" "What did you do together?" "Who was there?" "When did he get home?" You know what I ended up feeling? Like I'm a spy. If she hates him, why is she so interested in him? I think she's obsessed with him.'

How Conflict Affects Children

Children who are used in their parents' fighting develop emotional, behavioural, and social problems. If the fighting is severe and extends for a long time, children show their distress either in their behaviours (externalizing) or in their emotions (internalizing). Children who externalize their problems have difficulty with anger and aggression and in dealing with peers and adults. Children who internalize their problems are fearful, withdrawn, and uncommunicative, and anxious about expressing their feelings, and have somatic symptoms (Johnston et al., 1989).

Over the long term, if their distress is not attended to, these children can become more damaged. They become oppositional in their behaviour, and even conduct disordered. They have problems in school and/or with peers. Some of their symptoms are similar to those which children develop when they have post-traumatic stress disorder.

Children caught in their parents' fighting become overburdened with fear and anxiety about their parents (Wallerstein, 1985). Sad, vigilant, and depressed, they are overinvolved in their parents' lives as a heavy cost to their own.

What Conflict Does to the Emotional World of the Child

Children cannot tolerate being caught between their parents. To understand how this disturbs them, we will try to describe how it looks inside the child's mind: Children love their parents and want to stay close to them. When loving one gets them in trouble with the other, they are in a terrible bind. On the one hand, they do not want to lose their connection to both parents; on the other hand, they realize that if they don't choose one, they may lose both. Thus, 'If I love my mother, my father is mad. If I love my father, my mother is mad. I love both, but I might lose both if I keep loving both, so I'd better choose one.'

Another problem for the growing child arises when the parents view each other in black-and-white terms: 'I'm right, she's wrong,' 'I'm good, she's bad.' Children do not know how to handle these contradictions. Young children cannot hold two different points of view of the same person at the same time. They think: 'When I am with my mother, she's is a good person, but my father is bad. When I am with my father, he is a good person, but my mother is bad. Are there two mommies and two daddies?' Children cannot make the leap required to think, 'My mom and dad see each other as bad, but that does not mean the other parent is bad.' This last piece of reasoning is too sophisticated for a young child.

For older children, being caught between parents is unbearable. Their anxieties are so painful that they completely align with one parent against the other just to escape the terrible feeling of being caught. This is their solution to the 'loyalty conflict.'

What Is a Loyalty Conflict?

A loyalty conflict arises when a child feels that loving one parent gets him or her in trouble with the other. This is an impossible situation for a child because children love both parents. Children handle this loyalty conflict in different ways at different times depending on their stage of development (Johnston and Campbell, 1988).

Children between 2 and 4 show temporary intense distress, especially at transfers.

Children between 4 and 7 create alliances that shift back and forth between the parents. When they're with mom, she's right; when they're with dad, he's right. They do not try to make sense of these contradictions. Their alliances are not based on reasoning; they are just trying to stay close to both parents.

Children between 7 and 9 are more able to reason. They understand how they are placed in their parents' conflict, worry about it, and become very anxious. These children are genuinely anguished. They create alliances to escape from their anguish.

Children between 9 and 12, who are at the 'moral' stage of development, tend to form permanent alliances with the parent they think is right. Adolescents maintain permanent alliances and may completely reject one parent for a while. This may change when they are able to understand their parents' different points of view.

What It Feels Like to Be in a Loyalty Bind

When assessors interview parents who are at war, they get a feeling for what children caught in these disputes experience. As each parent tries to recruit the assessor, the assessor feels pulled in two different directions. The assessor knows that if she agrees with one parent, the other parent will be threatened and angry. She also knows that neither parent will tolerate her seeing things differently from them. *Disagreement is experienced as betrayal.* Each parent wants the assessor to agree with him *completely.* This is what makes custody-and-access work stressful: the constant threat of one or both parents becoming angry. It is like walking a tightrope – each parent is yanking the rope on which you are precariously balanced. This experience allows assessors to know how the child feels and what he needs.

'Walking on Eggshells'

'My 9-year-old stomps up the walk into the hall, slams the door, and gives me a hug. I hug him back. He breaks away. I can tell from the way he kicks the pillows in the living room that he's on edge. He's just back from a week-end with his dad. I know these transitions are hard for him, so I try to stay reasonable and consistent. Transitions must be a painful reminder to him that his family is broken. And on top of that, we, his parents, are still fighting after four years.

'What should I do? Give him space? He keeps doing things to provoke me, like throwing muddy shoes on the kitchen table.

'Connect with him? He snaps for me to leave him alone.

'Confront him? He's too fragile for that. He's already holding back tears.

'Half an hour later, the big explosion. Four-letter words and, "Dad lets me play videos at his house. I hate you. You're awful."

'I send him to his room. He gives me a look so full of frustration and anguish that it breaks my heart. I just want to pick him up and tell him everything will be all right. When he tells me how things are better at his dad's, I know he's just hurting, but I get scared. What if he won't love me as much? I feel like giving in to everything just so he'll love me. I know this is ridiculous, but when your child is away so much with the other parent, and you know the other parent is working overtime on alienating him from you, it's hard not to get pulled into "the Power Struggle with the Enemy."

'I have accepted that my son's father and I are trying to parent the same child, although we never speak. I have tried every form of help there is, but nothing works. If I talk to my ex, I get the same profanities I get from my son when he gets home: "You're a liar, you're selfish, you don't love me. You are ruining my life. You twist everything around." These are his dad's words and I remember them well.'

HOW CHILDREN MANAGE THEIR PARENTS' CONFLICT

Children who have to manage their parents' conflict find creative, but emotionally damaging, ways to deal with the impossible dilemma of being caught in the middle. The biggest fear a child has is to lose a parent.

Johnston and Campbell (1988) uncovered four ways that children try to manage their loyalty conflict.

1. Some children learn to manoeuvre between their battling parents. Because their parents are preoccupied with fighting, they tend to ignore their children's needs. So children learn different ways of manoeuvring in order to get what they need. Instead of asking for what they want, they become indirect and manipulative.

   Seven-year-old Michael would throw a temper tantrum every time he was asked to clean up his room, wash his hands for dinner, or help with household chores. His mother, worried about the pending court appearance, gave in to his demands instead of focusing on why his behaviour problems had suddenly escalated.

   Manoeuvring may get them what they want, but these children tend to become quite focused on themselves and fail to learn compassion and sensitivity to others.

2. Some children become experts at being cool and 'together,' and use *equilibrating* as a management strategy. They seem to see both sides of their parents' conflict. Nothing is a problem, and they have themselves and their lives under control. When interviewed about their parents, they talk like mini-lawyers or social workers, sounding very intellectual and carefully weighing the pros and cons of each parent's position.

   Nine-year-old Jenna spoke clearly about how she understood her father's sense of outrage at having to follow a schedule for visits; but she also empathized with her mother, who wanted a life of her own and didn't like her ex just dropping by. Jenna said that she didn't really know who was right, and added that she preferred to spend time on her own, working on hobbies and crafts.

   For these children, there is no safe place in the family to talk about their anxieties and feelings; so they learn to conceal them. They become prematurely self-reliant.

3. To sidestep fights and preserve their separate relationships with both parents, some children *merge*, or completely agree with whichever parent they are with.

When with her dad, 6-year-old Holly agreed with him that they didn't have enough time together; when with her mother, she agreed that the visits with her father were too long. Holly refused to acknowledge the contradictions between her parents, each of whom insisted she was on their side.

Because they are terrified of rejection, these children do not allow themselves to have an opinion of their own. They sacrifice their own feelings and views in order to merge with each parent and ensure these relationships continue.

Nine-year-old Tom and 7-year-old David had been interviewed so often by various social workers at the child welfare agency and the school board that by the time we interviewed them, we were not sure they were telling us what they were feeling. When they were with their mother, they complained about their father, and when they were with their father, they put down their mother. When with their parents, they denigrated the assessors. They were unreliable reporters of their own experience. They had been recruited so successfully into satisfying the contradictory needs of each parent, that they had lost sight of their own views and needs.

4. For some children, dealing with parents' fighting is so disorganizing that they fall apart emotionally, or *diffuse*. They become unhinged and emotionally disorganized.

Seven-year-old Peter had witnessed his parents' conflict for over two years since their abrupt and hostile separation. Every pick-up and drop-off was a battleground. Every phone call between his parents was tense and unpleasant. Parent night at school and the Holiday Concert inevitably led to fighting about who would go; if both showed up, he was humiliated by how they treated each other in front of his friends. Peter's school grades deteriorated, and eventually he developed the strange habit of pulling hard at his eyebrows and hair. He was referred for psychiatric assessment.

Mavis Hetherington (1989) also studied how children coped with their parents' conflict and found that children exposed to conflict tended to react in two different ways. Boys fell into the group that became aggressive and impulsive. They had trouble with their peers and with school. This was particularly so if their parents were neglectful or emotionally unavailable. Another group, composed of boys *and* girls, learned how to use their parents' disagreements for their own gain. They played parents off each other. They tended to gravitate toward those in power and were focused on the need to win power struggles.

Warning: children living in chronic conflict become disturbed.

PARENTAL ALIENATION SYNDROME

The term 'parental alienation syndrome' was coined by Dr Richard Gardner (1992), a child psychiatrist. In working with children caught in their parents' fights, he noticed that when one parent encouraged the child to reject the other parent, the child often did. With time, the child refused to visit the other parent. Parental alienation does not, of course, include those situations where children refuse to be with a parent who has abused and hurt them. Refusing access under these conditions is appropriate and to be expected.

In parental alienation syndrome, with little or no evidence a parent is convinced the child is better off without the other parent. The parent lets the child know that she hates the other parent. She does this either subtly, by her attitude, or overtly, through her behaviour and words. She conveys to the child her disgust with the other parent. The parent sending these messages to the child is called 'the alienating parent.' The alienating parent can be either parent, although it is more commonly the parent with whom the child lives. The other parent is called 'the alienated parent.'

Seven-year-old Vicki's father told her he would pick her up one hour later than the scheduled time. She told her mother, Eleanor, who immediately rolled her eyes, and in a tone of disgust exclaimed how irresponsible and immature her father was. Hadn't he always been late? And not just with visits, but with support payments and legal papers. He was the same jerk now as he was in the marriage. Nothing had changed. Vicky could go on the visit if she wanted to. The choice was hers, but Eleanor could not under-

stand how anyone could like anything about her ex. If he really cared about his children, he would not be changing plans all the time. Eleanor withdrew to the other room to sound off about her ex with her friend.

Vicki, feeling confused and distressed, was left alone to wait for her father. Why did he always have to cause so many problems for her mother?

To stay close to her mother, Vicki has almost no alternative but to identify with her mother's position and start blaming her father. Soon she will start withdrawing from him, and then at least her mother will be pleased with her.

When a parent withdraws or rejects the child whenever that child talks to the other parent, the child is given to understand that there is something very wrong with the other parent. She eventually starts believing it and acting like there is. She then often loses interest in the other parent.

Children in these situations may lose a parent altogether. Also, their overinvolvement with the remaining parent can result in emotional problems. Children in these situations learn that the love they receive is conditional on their agreeing with the alienating parent. Besides, they are dependent on that parent. When children always have to adjust their responses to a parent's, their growth and development become distorted. Parental alienation teaches children that they have no right to independent thoughts, are not important, and must cave in to the opinions of others.

Caught in these situations, children generally do not understand what is happening. Sometimes older children realize they have lost a parent and later, with sadness and anger, may reject the alienating parent. Sometimes, on their own, they seek out the alienated parent.

Disputes involving parental alienation require clinical assessment. If such disputes are assessed early in the process, there is some chance to resolve them. Once they are 'crystallized,' and the child is over 8 years old, it is much more difficult to reverse them.

Parental alienation syndrome develops easily in the emotionally unsettled period after separation. It does not spring up suddenly one day; rather, it arises slowly out of small, hardly significant behaviours: badmouthing, polarizing, manipulating, delaying, and so on. Over time, these behaviours add up to a corrosive family problem.

Parental alienation syndrome is misnamed: it should be called 'child alienation syndrome,' because it is really the child who becomes alienated.

Take the 'Am I Alienating My Child' Test

It is absolutely critical that you in no way do anything to create *this horrible situation for your child*. Not that you would deliberately do so. But it can arise from behaviours that you are not aware of, *so beware, and be aware*. For now, answer the following questions very honestly, and if you are not sure of the answers, consult with a trusted, objective friend. This is very, very important. Get a cup of coffee, study the list below, and check off any behaviours you do.

1. Denigrating the other parent.
2. Blaming the other parent.
3. Talking at length about the other parent, even if it is 'just explaining.'
4. Making excuses for the other parent.
5. Not insisting that the child spend time with the other parent by letting it be 'the child's choice.'
6. Not respecting the child's time with the other parent by being late, or early, or by not organizing what the child takes with him.
7. Not allowing for differences in parenting.
8. Trying to correct the other parent's parenting.
9. Telling the other parent how to parent.
10. Having a fight with your ex in front of the child.
11. Having a fight with your ex on the phone within the child's earshot.
12. Always adding your two cents to what the child says about the other parent.
13. Confirming the child's negative feelings about the other parent.
14. Not wanting to share the child.
15. Telling the child how much you miss him when he goes to the other parent.
16. Damning the other parent with faint praise.
17. Thinking you are the better parent.

18. Encouraging the child to have your point of view.
19. Rolling your eyes when the other parent's name is mentioned or when he is on the phone, or when he is late.
20. Explaining the problems between you and your ex in such a way that the child takes your side.
21. Giving the child information he should not have: knowledge about your fighting, your court proceedings, your finances, your shared past, the cause of the marital breakdown.
22. Making the child choose between you.
23. Making the child feel guilty for loving the other parent.
24. Setting up interesting activities when the child is going to the other parent's.

Important Note:
Some of the items on this list may seem small and insignificant (like No. 19), but the effect of these behaviours is cumulative. We should add here that married parents are at times similarly disrespectful with each other and are therefore just as damaging to their children. It is not good for children when parents, married or divorced, engage in power struggles.

If you have ticked off ten items on the list, you are on the way to seriously jeopardizing your child's attachment to the other parent.

- The best way to love your child is to support his love for the other parent. This teaches him to love you.
- When you undermine his love for the other parent, you are teaching him not to love *you*.

STOP THE BLAME!

Parental alienation syndrome is the final and most tragic result of blaming your spouse. You *must* come to understand why you are blaming. What use is it to you to place blame? We cannot resolve anything while we are blaming others. Blaming comes from not wanting to take responsibility. Blaming comes from being a child, not an adult. You want to grow up and take responsibility.

Take a look at why you blame, by filling in this questionnaire

The 'Stop the Blame' Questionnaire
Why Are You Disagreeing, Fighting, Getting into a Power Struggle?

1. What is the cause of the problems between you and your ex-spouse?
2. What is your part in these problems?
3. What do you do that pushes your spouse's buttons?
4. How does your spouse react when you push his/her buttons?
5. How do you wish your spouse would respond when you push his/her buttons?
6. How does s/he push your buttons?
7. How do you react when she/he pushes your buttons?
8. How do you wish you would respond when s/he pushes your buttons?
9. Why do you 'react' instead of 'responding'?

Reflection: 'What Do I Need to Learn about Myself?'

About the separation:

10. What has been the hardest part in your separation?
11. If you had to separate again, what would you do differently?
12. If you knew someone thinking of separating, what advice would you give?

About your childhood and the conflict you find yourself in now:

13. How did your parents fight? How did it feel?
14. What did they do that bothered you most?
15. How did this affect the way you hoped to raise your children?
16. How do your children react to your fights?
17. Which of their reactions worry you?
18. How does *your* way of handling conflict affect your children?

19. What is it in your children that makes it hard for them to handle your conflict?
20. What do you do that makes it harder for them?
21. What would you like to change in how you handle your ex?
22. How could you try to protect your children from the conflict?
23. How do you make sure your children are not in a loyalty conflict between you and your ex?

Rating your answers

Answering these questions should highlight for you your part in the conflict with your ex. Some of the childhood questions should help you see where some of your patterns come from.

For instance, your answer to the first question was probably about your ex. However, the answer to the second question was only about you. If you could not answer it, you need to get to know more about yourself. While there are conflicts in which only one parent is the problem, usually the conflict involves both parents. Parents in conflict believe that the other parent is the sole cause of the problem. This is one of the distinguishing characteristics of high-conflict couples.

Questions 3 to 7 test your awareness of your personality, and your ex's.

Questions 8 and 9 allow you some distance from your behaviour. When you learn to distance yourself, change becomes possible.

Questions 10 to 12 allow for learning from your separation.

Questions 13 and 14 should elicit patterns from when you were younger, and give you some ideas about why you think and react the way you do.

Question 15 shows you your hopes for bringing up your children.

Questions 16 to 18 refocus you on how your children experience your conflict.

Question 19 to 23 are about possible ways you can change things to help your children. This is the *hope*: this is where to *concentrate your energies.*

Children's Reactions to Parental Conflict

Developmental stage	Cognitive development	Reactions	Ways to help
Toddlers (18 months to 3 years)	They respond to the body language of conflict. Children are sensitive to the stress of the conflict but do not understand its content. They may think they did something to cause the parents to be angry.	Children may appear anxious or distressed in response to conflict. Their insecurity may result in clingy behaviour, wide-eyed staring, crying, and temper tantrums.	Avoid arguing and heated discussions in front of the children. If child witnesses your conflict, stop the fight and say you are sorry to be frightening him. Reassure the child that both of you still love him and that you are not angry with him.
Preschoolers (3 to 5 years)	Preschoolers are concrete thinkers, meaning that they interpret events and explanations literally. Children are very 'me focused'; they view themselves as the cause of what happens around them.	Preschoolers are very aware of changes in family routines and structure, and cry or are unusually oppositional at the changes. They may regress to more immature behaviour in the face of major changes. They may bedwet, be clingy, and cry.	Minimize the number of changes in routines to which the child must adapt. Reassure the child that she is not responsible for the conflict. Tell the child that the conflict is a problem for the adults to solve.

Early school-age years (6 to 8 years)	These children can understand more complicated explanations, but have difficulty thinking about two different points of view at the same time. They may be fearful of losing their parents, and try to please each of them in different ways.	They have concerns about having their needs looked after (physical safety, food, etc.).	They may feel responsible for their parents' conflict. They may try to console/comfort their parents. They may 'parrot' explanations or blaming statements they have heard from their parents: 'It's your fault Mommy is sad.' They may ask the same questions repeatedly: 'Who will look after me? Is Mommy coming back?'	They experience 'shifting alliances,' taking sides first with one parent and then the other. They tell each parent what the parent wants to hear: 'It's no fun at Dad's house.'	Acknowledge to the child how hard it is to have Mom and Dad not getting along. Offer repeated reassurances that the child will be looked after and will not lose either parent. Reassure the child that he does not have to choose sides for you to love him. Reassure the child that even if you do not agree on some things, it is okay for her to have a relationship with both of you.

Children's Reactions to Parental Conflict (*Continued*)

Developmental stage	Cognitive development	Reactions	Ways to help
Early school-age years (6 to 8 years) (*continued*)	Children are very sensitive to conflict.	They may put themselves in the middle of your conflict to stop you from fighting.	Thank the child for trying to help but reassure him that it is not his job to stop the conflict.
	Child's own distress may come out in school or with friends because child does not feel he can safely express it at home.	There may be a decline in school performance.	Give the child permission to talk about her distress.
		They may have conflict with friends or teachers.	Let her know you can handle her feelings, which will not make you *sad* or *mad*.
		They may be more withdrawn with their parents and family.	Listen to and accept the child's experience of your divorce, even if it is different from your own.
Older school-age (9 to 12 years)	These children can think in more abstract terms.	They are very aware of changes in family.	Offer neutral, non-blaming explanations to questions.
	They may want more details about the nature of the conflict.	They may form a 'permanent alliance,' siding with one of you against the other.	Remind her that she does not have to choose sides.
			Encourage him to be open to other parent.

They can listen to explanations and take a position on who and what to believe.	They seldom change their mind about their alliance.	Unless there are safety issues, support contact with other parent.
They may feel distressed about the separation, or relieved if the parental relationship was destructive.	They may refuse to see one of you.	Encourage her to express her feelings and concerns.
	They may be angry or aloof.	Listen and empathize with the child's point of view.
	Their school work may suffer.	Reassure her that the adults are working on ways of resolving the conflict.
	If they are relieved about the divorce, it may result in improvement in school/social functioning.	
The teenage years (13 to 18 years)		
Teens are able to think about parents' different points of view without taking sides.	While still distressed about the separation, they are able to understand reasons leading to changes in family.	Without blaming, talk to your teenagers about your separation.
They want to know 'the truth' and think independently.	The stress of separation may exacerbate the volatile emotions that are normal in adolescence (argumentative, angry).	Explain why you are separating, and take responsibility for your part in the break-down of the relationship.
They are better able to use friends and outsider interests as a buffer against sadness and distress regarding separation.	They may spend more time with friends and at activities outside the family.	Acknowledge that your separation will challenge their beliefs in the permanency of relationships.

Children's Reactions to Parental Conflict (*Concluded*)

Developmental stage	Cognitive development	Reactions	Ways to help
The teenage years (13 to 18 years) (*continued*)	They are able to manage changes in routines/ schedules.	They are likely to side against the parent who caused the separation.	Acknowledge that while there will be changes, she will not lose either parent and does not have to choose sides. Acknowledge that the divorce comes at a very bad time for him. Acknowledge that you know even though he is a teenager, he still needs support and encouragement from both of you.

C.B. Garrity and M.A. Baris, 1994, 29–37. Adapted.

11. Traditional Custody and Access Arrangements

WHAT TO EXPECT AND HOW TO MAKE IT WORK

If you have a more traditional arrangement, with your children living primarily with one of you (the residential parent) and visiting with the other (the nonresidential parent), you need to prepare yourself for a period of adjustments, both practical and emotional. You will have to come to terms with major changes in your living situation, and a new routine with your children.

If you are the nonresidential parent, your friends and relatives may become angry and upset on your behalf. Increasingly, as grandparents receive formal recognition in parenting plans and legal arrangements, their opinions and preferences will influence your views and attitudes. It is important not to allow your family and friends' support for you to turn you against your spouse. These triangles easily develop and then deteriorate into what Johnston and Campbell (1988), call 'tribal warfare' with both parents' social networks intensifying the bitterness of your conflict.

Beware of wanting to retaliate against your spouse – this is always a recipe for disaster. Your mantra has to be this: 'What is best for my child?' Let this be your benchmark question. Ask yourself often. If you are doing what is right for your child, you are doing what is right.

Adjustments

Separated parents in more traditional arrangements face many practical and administrative challenges, such as arranging for the legal separation, dividing property and assets, establishing a parenting plan, and changing residences, schools, and sometimes work. Most separated parents face economic hardship: setting up two homes is expensive. Being a residential parent means you initially have a lot of unforeseen expenses.

Financial Issues

Nonresidential parents often find that paying child support and covering their own daily costs are enormous financial adjustments. The federal government has established guidelines for child support payments that leave very little control in the hands of either parent. Depending on your income and the number of children in your family, as the nonresidential parent you will be asked to pay a certain portion of your monthly income in child support (Federal Child Support Guidelines, May 1997).

Post-divorce financial arrangements are a magnet for anger, bitterness, and hostility. Many of us are irrational when it comes to money anyway. Even though you love your children and want to support them, being told exactly how much you have to pay brings out the rebel in many of us: 'No-one is going to take my hard earned money just like that.' You feel rebellious. On top of this, for many parents the monthly amount seems substantial. Even though you love your children, you may resent the financial stress. You may find that the financial stress increases your anger toward your ex-partner, even though it was not he or she who established the guidelines. And the money is for your children.

Besides all this, you may resent 'the way she is spending your money.' You may feel like withholding support in order to exert some control over how the money is spent, or maybe just control over your ex-partner (with whom you are angry anyway).

Be very careful here. *Beware and be aware*. This is an explosive topic for everyone, so you have to stay cool. This is a time for that calming *self-talk*. It is important to separate out these resentments from your love and care for your children. Your children continue to need your emotional *and* financial support to cope with the hardships at hand. You want to do all you can to make them safe, settled, and secure.

For them and the other parent to have enough financial resources makes the difference between living in anxiety and fear, and living a secure, well-planned life. Children sense when their parents are worrying about money, and they feel bad about needing the material things that are causing their parents anxiety. All of this suggests why you need to discipline your resentments. One of the fathers in the group said, 'I say to myself, "Harry, just don't go down that road to resentment and bitterness, you know there is no turn off."' There is no point using support payments as a weapon against your spouse, because the one who will suffer is your child. Children pay for your resentments through their quality of life. It costs money to have a rich and varied life, and only a varied life develops a child's many talents.

A successful computer consultant, David, and his wife, Jennifer, agreed that she would have sole custody of their children, Mike, 9, and Melissa, 11, because he travelled extensively in his work. Despite considerable conflict before their separation, they very co-operatively settled their parenting plan and financial issues, including child support. They had minimal contact with one another. When David was in town, he spent as much time as possible with the children.

One day, when he picked them up at their home, he noticed that the children were dressed in expensive clothes and that the house had been redecorated. He especially noticed the 33-inch TV. He got mad, instantly: 'How come she is spending my money on furnishings and clothes? She should be getting the kids into sports and activities. I don't want them lolling around watching TV all day – I want them out there! I want them to succeed in life! What the hell is she up to?'

Instead of practising calming self-talk, or exploratory communication with Jennifer, David's resentment simmered, and he delayed his support payments. Eventually he withheld them altogether, which escalated the conflict between himself and Jennifer. But worst of all, the children were not enrolled in summer camp or swimming lessons because there was no money in the till. With no activities over the summer months, they were left to watch TV, which was, of course, David's worst nightmare. When he saw that, he was more open to the lawyers' joint proposal that he resume payments, and that he and Jennifer agree on what their children need.

Adjusting to Restricted Time with Your Children

While there is an growing trend toward increased shared parenting arrangements, after separation two thirds of children still live primarily with the mother. Often this is voluntary, sometimes it is imposed (Maccoby & Mnookin, 1992). The implications of this can be profound for nonresidential parents who must adapt to a new relationship with their children.

If you spend about the same amount of time with your children now as you did when you were living together, then your adjustment is not so difficult. For example, if you spent considerable daily time with your children prior to your separation, and you still do so after your separation, you may experience less of a sense of loss. If, on the other hand, you are not able to be with your children every day, even if this is for practical and justifiable reasons, you are going to experience more intense feelings of loss. The most difficult adjustment relates to those situations where you have no choice but to have much reduced time with your children, for reasons that you feel are unjustified.

Living as the Residential Parent

Because residential parents have their children living with them, they feel some compensation for the loss of the family. Residential parents, speak of the enormous pleasure they derive from having their children around to love and enjoy. They love being with them, taking part in their daily lives, and witnessing their day-to-day struggles and achievements.

But these parents also comment on the burden of parenting alone. Weekdays are hectic; many mothers must work and balance time with their children and extended family, while trying to develop a new life. Weekends are rushed, because in the more traditional arrangement these parents have only every second weekend to enjoy 'fun' time with their children. Out of necessity, mothers have to distribute household tasks to their children.

The Need for Comfort

It can be lonely being the only parent in the house, with no one you can consult. Being lonely, residential parents often find themselves confiding in their children. They find it easy and satisfying to do so. Be aware, however, that often in the post-separation transition, parents turn to their children for comfort now and then, and then suddenly it becomes a habit, as much for them as for their children. The children become little, responsible 'substitute spouses.' Children, especially over 7 years of age, are particularly adept at empathizing with their parents, and parents can find it tempting to draw on their resources. Similarly, some parents allow or encourage their younger children to sleep with them as a comfort to the parents during their adjustment. Some of this is an understandable temporary reaction to grieving; but if extended, it encourages an unhealthy dependency between parent and child.

When parents rely too much on their children for emotional support, it is called 'parentification of children' – a process whereby children, in response to the cues their parents give, begin to take care of their parents. This is not damaging in the short run, but can be in the long run. It turns children into caretakers. They learn to take care of other peoples' pain instead of paying attention to their own. Children need their parents to help them deal with the pain of family disruption; similarly, parents need appropriate adult supports to take care of their own pain.

When they separate, residential parents also experience the stress of sudden economic hardship. If you have been a stay-at-home parent, you may need to find employment and move into a smaller home, often in a less desirable neighbourhood. As well, your children often have to change schools. All these unpleasant 'forced' changes come at a time when you and your children are already overtaxed by the emotional burden of adjusting to family disruption. What you all need is stability, familiarity, and routine – not more changes.

Research shows that a child's adjustment to divorce is greatly influenced by the psychological and emotional well-being of the parent with whom he lives most of the time (Kline et al., 1989; Guidubaldi & Perry, 1985; Johnston et al., 1989). Children are well when their parents are; or, to put it negatively, children who are living with an overwhelmed and emotionally unavailable parent find it harder to adjust.

The irony is that just when your children need you most, you are most likely to be emotionally and physically less available, because you yourself are overtaxed by all you are going through and all you have to do. It is a real struggle to stay available to your children – to tune in to their distress when you yourself need a break.

You Need to Support the Nonresidential Parent–Child Relationship

Because of your influence over the child, how you view the child's relationship with the other parent has a considerable impact on that relationship. As the nonresidential parent, your ability to create and maintain a strong, child-focused relationship with the child is also critical. Here you and your ex must work together.

Research shows that without the residential parent's support, the child's relationship with the nonresidential parent suffers (Guidubaldi & Perry, 1985; Kurdek, 1988). If both parents support the non-residential parent's carefully established relationship with the child, the child is in good shape to preserve and maintain good relationships with both parents.

Supporting your child's relationship with the other parent may at times prove difficult for you. As the residential parent you have a lot on your plate. You do most of the caretaking of the children, so you probably feel depleted. Sometimes it seems like you are doing the day-to-day grind, and that the other parent has the easy part. You have days when you resent being the disciplinarian or 'the bad guy,' while your ex-partner, 'the good guy,' gets recreational time with the kids. You do all the work while he has all the fun.

'I'm frustrated that their father won't even pay regular child support and yet when he's with the kids he is Santa Claus, all gifts and fun. The kids think he's great! He's the bearer of gifts. He has wheels and money to spend.'

Besides, the children are upset and stressed with all they are going through. They are either clamouring for their father, clinging to you, or just feeling terrible that the family is no longer together. They are demanding extra time and care just when you need time and care yourself. You are just barely managing, day to day, with what you have to do, so how are you supposed to support the child's relationship with his father? It feels like too much of an imposition for you to have to worry about that. Besides, the conflict between you and your spouse has already eroded much of your good will toward him, and you may not feel like 'doing him a favour.' With all that he's put you through, it's just easier to let him fend for himself. You feel like pretending he just does not exist.

It is understandable for you to feel these things, but *stop and think.* Take time for some good self-talk. Our experience is that separated parents feel these resentments mainly in the early months after the separation. After that, they slowly begin to work things out. Only then do they start reaping the benefits of co-operative parenting. Benefits like being able to share the emotional, physical, and financial burdens of parenting. This is a long-term benefit that you do not want to jeopardize by giving vent, too soon, to momentary frustrations.

Don't blow long-term gain for short-term pain.

Helping your children have a good connection to their father is not doing *him* a favour – it is doing *your children* a favour. Kids do better when they are well connected to both parents. And most of all, when you have happy children, *your* life is easier.

Getting Along with Your Ex

There are built-in liabilities to being the residential parent. Because you do not see what is going on in the other home, and because when relations are tense you cannot always check things out, you have to make certain assumptions about what is going on in his home. *Assume the best and do not immediately jump to negative conclusions.*

Assuming the best takes considerable self-discipline, but it is worth it. When things go wrong, you can tell yourself to relax, that there is a reasonable explanation for events. When you hear worrisome things from your children, you can remind yourself that children caught in conflicts are often storytellers. They often say negative things to each parent about the other. This kind of calming self-talk pays off in good relationships and increased co-operation.

Becoming negative and suspicious is too easy and leads to bad attitudes. You and your ex can end up in a negative cycle. You can get suspicious, and start competing with him. When you do this, everything turns into a problem – for instance, when your son comes home from a pleasant weekend with his father, you can choose to see it as your loss rather than his gain. You can get jealous of his good time. Or you can worry that your son loves his dad more than you. This can develop into a power struggle – at least – in your own mind – about which of you will win your son's affection and loyalty. You can start to attribute negative motives to the other parent – for instance, you can say to yourself that he wants time with his son, not because he loves his son, but because he wants to hurt you. You start thinking that he wants to be with his children just to make your life difficult. Eventually you start seeing your son's time with his father not as the child's right, but as yours to control. This is a bad cycle to spin into.

Our experience shows that many parents have these unproductive thoughts, and that the ones who manage best are the ones who put them aside and stay focused on their children's needs.

Expect That You and Your Ex Will Not See Eye to Eye

It is common for separated mothers and fathers to report very different perceptions of the same events, particularly about time spent with their children. Braver and his colleagues (1991) found that residential mothers tended to report that fathers spent less time with their children than what was reported by the fathers; while fathers reported mothers interfering with their time with their children more often than did the mothers. The authors concluded that 'asking divorced parents the same question garners two very different responses.'

Instead of trying to convince your ex-partner that he or she is wrong, just expect to see things differently. It is probably because of irresolvable differences that you have separated, so let it go. Focus on what you *can* agree on, which is usually the huge and important fact that you both love your child and want what is best for her.

Visualize Your Ex as a Parent, Not a Spouse

The role of a parent is different from that of a spouse. This is a big adjustment to make. Your spouse has let you down, which is why you separated. But it does not mean that he or she is going to disappoint the children. While there may be parenting problems in the first months, up to two or three years after the divorce, research suggests that many parents' skills improve in the long run (Kelly, 1993). Some parents become better parents, some parents become worse. It remains to be seen. The best thing you can do is support the child's relationship with the other parent; that way, if it flounders you won't be able to blame yourself for having hurt your child.

Why Help the Other Parent Be a Good Parent Now?

This is an important question, which we will examine from different perspectives. First we'll look at reasons to preserve this relationship; then we examine reasons not to. Some parents improve as parents after separation, because their parenting is no longer undermined by difficulties in the marital relationship. Also, when two adults are parenting together, often one functions better than the other. When they separate, the underfunctioning one becomes more competent as a parent. Also, keeping both parents involved with the children allows for another home in case of emergency. If something were to happen to you, the children would have another parent. And remember, as well, that children whose fathers remain involved, both emotionally and financially, pursue higher levels of education and achieve better careers (Bisnaire et al., 1990).

Encouraging children to know their parents is crucial, because children always yearn to know their parents. This seems to be a biologically encoded longing. Children who are deprived of contact with a parent often idealize the lost parent and blame themselves, and the parent with whom they are living, for that loss. When children idealize an absent parent, they are at risk for developing blind spots in their interpersonal relationships. It is as if they cannot properly evaluate people because they idealize them. When they grow up, they are often not realistic in their choice of life partners.

Unless they are at risk from the other parent, despite any and all shortcomings you may see in that parent, it is better for children to make their own decisions of exclusion, and to do so later in their lives, than for you to do it for them now. As they grow older, children will view the situation from their own perspective, and may well resent you for having restricted their relationship with their father or mother. This resentment can undermine your own relationship with your children, and you will be the loser. It can cause a rift that you may not be able to mend. Besides, you can never make up to a child for time lost with the other parent.

Now for the *negatives*. There are some relationships between children and parents that are destructive to children. Are these worth encouraging? It depends on the nature and degree of the destructiveness, and especially on the attitude of the offending parent. It is always best for the child if the offending parent can be made to see the damage he or she has caused the child, and to take responsibility and make changes. We examine these situations closely in Chapter 13. If a parent hurts a child and will not take responsibility for it and rectify it, that parent's time with the child will need to be restricted.

LIVING AS THE NONRESIDENTIAL PARENT

More often than not it is fathers who assume the role of nonresidential parent. Whether you are a mother or a father, being a nonresidential parent is an enormous change in the way you live and relate to your children.

Nonresidential parents, and their children, feel the shock of the separation at the point in time when the parent physically moves out of the family home. Until that point, the separation is just an idea. But when moving day arrives, the divorce becomes a reality. Fathers often feel disoriented once they lose the day-to-day company of their children. They suddenly lose their secure identity as parents; for them, being a parent was associated with being a live-in parent.

As one father said, 'I am not a part-time father. I'm a full-time father who sees his children part-time.' This is a powerful summarization of the nonresidential parent's new dilemma. Sadly, no part-time relationship can replace the intimacy of a live-in relationship.

Father's Grief

In his 1993 book *Divorce and Disengagement*, Edward Kruk provides an extensive overview of the impact of divorce on father–child relationships. Fathers (or mothers, if they are nonresidential parents) who have been closely involved with their children experience very painful grief when threatened with restricted time with their children. A key worry for fathers is that they may lose their relationship with their children altogether. If this perceived threat is high, fathers themselves develop physical or mental health problems, such as ulcers or depression.

Research by Greif (1979) shows that fathers suffer because in addition to losing their families, they often lose their support networks and have difficulty establishing new relationships. This loneliness, or pining, combined with the loss of daily contact with their children, can lead fathers to experience profound feelings of loss. It is these painful feelings associated with 'child absence' that sometimes cause them to pull away from their children. They cannot handle the pain – and often these are the fathers who had been the most closely involved with the children before the separation. When they pull away from their children, it is a tragedy for the child as well as the family. Kruk (1992) emphasizes the importance of fathers successfully completing the grieving process so that they can preserve and maintain their relationships with their children.

It is important for you to express your grief so that it does not interfere with your relationship with your children. You have to accept the fact that you can no longer have a live-in, full-time relationship with your children, and you have to grieve this terrible loss. Grieving releases the energy you will need to create a new and different relationship with your children – one that is not based on a full-time live-in arrangement.

You may need to find a safe place to deal with the new realities of your life: the pain you feel when you pick up and drop off your children, your loneliness, your longing to be with them, and the daily reminders of the dreadful change in your role as a parent. You may need to speak to a therapist or a support group, or to a trustworthy, experienced friend – preferably one who has already navigated these troubled waters. You will need to explore new strategies for staying close to your children and new ways to be a strong presence in their lives. If you do not grieve your very considerable losses, you risk not getting up close and personal with your children. Pain that you do not feel and express, at least to yourself, interferes with your ability to be close to your children (or anyone else, for that matter).

Creating Closeness

Creating and maintaining closeness with your child when you are not living with him is a whole new ball game. Some fathers find it challenging, others find it downright difficult. It is definitely a different skill than the one you needed when you were living with your children. When you live with your children you have all sorts of opportunities for closeness built right into the living situation. You take it for granted; it does not need to be created.

'I nearly died when I realized I had to make conversation with Doug [6 years old]. I used to just be there when he got home from school. I'd get home early from work twice a week so we could hang out. We had lots to say 'cause I knew everything he was into. Now I see him so sparely, that I am not tuned in to what he is doing and feeling. I'm in a sweat after we're together – it is such hard work to keep it going. It breaks my heart when I remember how close and easy it used to be. I don't think it will ever be the same again.'

Creating a Home

Some fathers find it taxing to create a home, cook meals and do the household chores. This is particularly true if your pre-separation arrangement was a more traditional one where these tasks were performed by the mother. While you are still reeling from the shock of your separation is not a good time to remember all the details involved in setting up a home for you and your children. That being said, some fathers relish setting up new family routines and rituals. It allows them to take charge of their time with their children and to spend one-to-one time with them in a warm, meaningful way.

Handling Distressed Children as Well as Your Own Distress

A major adjustment for you as a nonresidential parent is having to handle the fact that your children are upset because you are not living together. Your children are distressed, and they need your help to deal with it. Many fathers feel awkward about 'doing the feeling thing with the kids.' But you have to do it, because children do best when they can talk about their feelings. You should share your feelings with them too. Tell them how much you miss them, how hard it is not seeing them. But be careful not to make them feel guilty, because children are very vulnerable to feeling their parents' pain. There are two reasons why you want them to know you miss them: so that they know you love them and did not 'leave them'; and to encourage them to speak freely to you about their feelings.

If you are not comfortable discussing your and their emotions, seek out training in communication. It is the best investment you will ever make because communication is necessary for creating intimacy. This skill is going to be crucial in your new situation. You will encounter many tricky problems requiring careful, skillful emotional discussions. These discussions will be particularly demanding for you as the nonresidential parent because you will not have the luxury of extended, loose time with your children in which to discuss things in an unhurried way. You must make good use of the time you have with them.

Encourage your children to express their grief, even though it will bring up your own. Sharing your grief will bring you closer.

After he moved out, George was devastated and lonely. Seeing his son at scheduled times was so restrictive, he just wanted to 'walk away.' In therapy, George expressed his anguish. He was encouraged to think about how 6-year-old Bob would feel if he left. Chastened, he realized he was thinking only of himself and not thinking about his son. Next time he saw Bob, he reached out to him and asked him how his leaving the house affected him. Bob looked sad and asked his dad if he had moved out because of something he, Bob, had done: 'Was I bad?' George was taken aback at the question. He was shocked to realize what his son was thinking and suddenly understood how much he was hurting. He put his arms around him, reassured him that he had nothing to do with his leaving, and told him how much he missed him.

They discussed how often they would see each other and what they would do together. Bob wanted to go camping and fishing. He also wanted his father to read him his favourite story, 'just like we always did.' George felt moved and comforted by his talk with his son.

Unprocessed Grief Turns to Resentment

Even if you have agreed to a traditional arrangement, with the children living primarily with their mother, once you start 'visiting' them you can start to feel as if you are on the outside of their lives, with little control or influence over them. This can be devastating. Seeing them in such small stretches of time, you can worry that you'll lose your closeness to them. You may start envying the time their mother has with them and your heart turns to stone. You may feel resentful of her daily contact with them. If there is hostility between you and their mother, and you feel that the parenting arrangement is unfair to you, you may start telling yourself she is doing all she can to keep the children from you. You may feel jealous, disadvantaged, and victimized.

If you do not nip these negative thoughts in the bud, you will soon be wanting to retaliate. You may then start badmouthing her to your children, or taking them home late. You may feel angry enough to fight or sad enough to give up. You may find yourself reacting to situations and frustrations in a much more hostile way than is characteristic for you.

Tommy, 7, was very close to his mother and father. There was a growing bitterness in the marriage. Tommy, oldest of the three and a sensitive boy, and was given to worry. He was anxious about his connection to his parents. When they separated, his father – usually a peaceful and calm man –

became explosive and pounded on the front door when he could not see his children. His mother, a rational and intelligent woman, had changed the locks on the advice of her lawyer.

She had been frightened because her husband threatened her when she asked him to leave. In the clinical assessment, he said he could not live without his children. He saw no way to continue his closeness with them.

Tommy was agonized for himself, but more for his father. He adored his father and was anxious about his father's loss as well as his own: 'My daddy will die without me. He has to have as much time with me as possible.' Fortunately, when his parents heard what Tommy said, they realized their conflict had been more painful for Tommy than they thought and that they had been hurting Tommy. Through counselling, the couple dealt with feelings between them and developed a parenting plan to preserve the closeness of the children and parents.

What You Can Do to Ease Your Children's Pain

You see the pain and grief of your children and feel powerless to help. Fortunately, there is much you can do to ease your children's distress. To begin, you must take hold of your angry, destructive thinking through comforting self-talk. Tell yourself that you can develop whatever kind of relationship you want – that you are in control of that through the love you show your children. Remember that your children love you both and that no one but you can change that. Then get help to grieve. Develop a consistent, businesslike relationship with your ex that supports your children's relationship with both of you. Reassure your children of your love. Prove your love through consistent visits and good parenting and by not criticizing your ex. We repeat: during this period, *consistent* efforts are needed by both parents, and their extended families, to keep fathers closely involved with their children.

Many fathers do not make the difficult transition from live-in to visiting parent. Research shows that about one-third of noncustodial parents in nondisputing couples stopped visiting their children an average of four-and-a-half years after separation (Furstenberg & Cherlin, 1991). Even when regular access was recommended, two years after the clinical assessment, one-third of the nonresidential parents in conflicted divorces no longer visited their children (Radovanovic et al., 1994).

- It is worth every effort you expend to help stabilize your relationship with your child.
- Instead of wasting energy being angry or sad at the changes, get as close as you can to your child, who needs you more than ever right now.

Why Do Some Children Lose Contact with the Nonresidential Parent?

Researchers have found several reasons why children lose contact with the nonresidential parent: hostility between parents (Furstenberg & Cherlin, 1991; Wallerstein & Kelly, 1980; Kruk, 1993); remarriage by a parent (Furstenberg & Cherlin, 1991); and the voluntary withdrawal of some parents who cannot handle the grief of restricted time with their children (Kruk, 1992). Also, a certain percentage of parents simply pull away for reasons pertaining to themselves and their inability to see themselves as parents.

Fathers report that the hostility of their ex-partner, and their own difficulties in making the transition from the full caretaking role, were major factors influencing their ablility to grieve the loss of their day-to-day relationships with their children. When fathers are met with hostility every time they collect their children, they may withdraw to protect themselves.

Ted said, 'Every time I picked her up, her mother was throwing daggers at me in the background. I felt a scab being pulled off a wound that would never heal. After a while, despite my guilt, I stopped visiting her. I just couldn't take it.'

Some fathers withdraw because they are themselves children of divorce, and so do not appreciate how their withdrawal hurts their children. They have not sufficiently allowed themselves to experience the effect on their own lives of their father's abandonment. Some fathers lack the self-esteem to keep a good connection to their children. This is especially true right after the separation, when fathers themselves are depleted and grieving. Sometimes the father still loves his ex, and finds regular contact with her during transfers too painful to endure, and stops seeing his children because of this.

There are some fathers who only want to be with their children to stay in touch with the mother. This is not a good dynamic for the children, and can become dangerous for the ex-spouse. A child needs to know that the father wants to be with her because he loves her – not because she is a bridge to the mother. Fathers with this motivation often harass their ex-wives. They harass because they cannot accept that the spousal relationship is over and that they have to grieve the loss. They use their connection with the children to avoid facing that the spousal relationship has ended.

George called his ex almost every second day to discuss one thing or another. During these phone calls, he often wept and begged his ex-wife, Sylvia, to return to him. He seemed to have unlimited time to devote to his pursuit of Sylvia and was driving her crazy. He also cross-examined his daughter about every detail of Sylvia's life. When picking up his daughter, George lingered at his ex-wife's apartment, commenting on changes in the decor or furniture. Sylvia, irritated by the personal nature of his comments, assumed a cold, detached demeanour to try to discourage his approaches. George redoubled his efforts to reach Sylvia. During these transfers, 7-year-old Susan became sullen and defiant.

STRUCTURED TIME SHARING

Parents in amicable and disengaged separations are able to be flexible and spontaneous in their arrangements; those who are in conflict usually are not. Because your anger with each other threatens to erupt whenever you see or talk to each other, you need structure, as well as restricted time in each other's presence. Time sharing in these circumstances is one of the biggest challenges.

We now return to some of the guidelines for time sharing that we first discussed in Chapter 7. But we will adjust them to the requirements of high-conflict divorces. In these divorces the shape of time sharing depends on the age of the child, on where the parents live, *and* on the level of conflict between them. Because infants and toddlers need predictable routines, familiar surroundings, and intense closeness with one parent, visits with the other parent and/or the grandparents are usually shorter and more frequent – perhaps two visits a week of a few hours' duration. The age at which a child can manage overnights varies (see Chapter 7). It is then common to move on to less frequent visits – for example, alternating weekends and midweek access.

Given that parents move because of employment or other circumstances, it is not uncommon for parents to live far from one another. In such cases, geography often dictates the shape of the schedule. The lower the conflict in the parental relationship, the more flexibility the parents can handle, because they can communicate without anger and have the good will to accommodate each other. But even in friendly situations, parents' work schedules, and their new partners and families, complicate scheduling and make changes difficult to organize.

What Regular Visits Mean to the Child

Parents must remember that just as *their* time with the child is sacred, so also is the other parent's. And most of all, *the child's time with both parents is sacred*. Respecting the other parent's time is a way of saying to the child, 'Your father/mother is a person worthy of love and respect, and therefore so are you.' Keeping to the schedule is the most important way you put into practice the promise you as parents made to love your child, even though you no longer love each other. When you disrespect the schedule you are showing your child that his other parent is unworthy, and that by definition so is he. You are also showing him that he cannot trust you to put yourself aside for his needs.

Teresa, 9, told her counsellor, 'I know my mom thinks my dad is a jerk, because she always keeps him waiting. The other day, she cancelled my time with him just because she wanted to take me to her friends' cottage. I didn't say anything because I didn't want to spoil her fun, or make her mad, but I missed daddy. I'm starting to think the break-up was all her fault!'

Making Changes to the Schedule

In situations of low to middling conflict, it is better to keep the schedule structured and to request very few changes. In high-conflict situations, and in those where there is a history of aggression between parents, heavily structured schedules are required to prevent parental contact altogether. Children become extremely stressed when they witness parental conflict or are fearful about a parent's safety. These situations are discussed in more depth in Chapter 13.

Some changes, every now and then, cannot be avoided. But making them too often is asking for trouble. It creates, first, insecurity in the child's relationship with the other parent, and then, if changes continue, resentment. If changes persist, they eventually create insecurity in your relationship with the child. Parents should also refrain from making sudden requests for changes. Changes that are necessary must be discussed ahead of time, with offers for compensatory time. Any changes you ask for should, on the whole, be for reasons that benefit the child. And you need to reciprocate in kind. Self-centred reasons for making changes eventually wear out the other's good will.

TIPS FOR TIME-SHARING

1. Should You Arrange Telephone Access?

In friendly situations, liberal telephone contact is a benefit to everyone. It has a way of making the separated family feel like a viable unit. When you are able to tolerate and even enjoy your children contacting the other parent on 'your' time, you are giving your children a real gift.

But if there are hostilities between you, problems with telephone access can increase them, and frequent telephone calls are not usually manageable. They may feel intrusive and even harassing to you when you have the child with you. When you already feel you have too little time with your child, phone calls 'on your time' may upset you. Despite yourself, you may feel that the other parent is 'stealing' your time, or imagine that the other parent is trying to take the child from you or even check up on you. During the emotionally unsettled time immediately after separation, your feelings are more volatile than usual.

If you do agree to phone calls, scheduling them is tricky, because this can impose restrictions on children – especially older ones.

Eileen, 14, complained that although she loved her father, she found his phone calls every two days a 'bind' because she resented having to be home at 8:30 those nights.

If you agree to phone calls but secretly resent them, or if you are only complying because the court ordered them, you can inadvertently communicate your irritation to the child. The child is then placed in an awkward position. He wants to talk to the other parent, but he also wants to accommodate your preferences. He is in a bind: he wants to talk, and he does not want to talk. Caught in this way, a child can suddenly 'turn cold' to the parent on the phone, or cut a call short, or even refuse to come to the phone. Or the child may overreact by suddenly talking up a storm to the parent on the phone. So do not agree to phone calls unless you can handle them without hurting your child.

Scheduling phone calls requires careful thought, as well as cooperation between you and your ex. Even when planned, you can still sometimes be taken by surprise at the irrationality of your responses. Once again, careful inner dialogue helps you manage these tricky situations.

Although she knew that 9-year-old Trevor was excited to hear from his father, Susan dreaded hearing her ex-partner's voice when he called every other night at 7:30. She delayed picking up the telephone and sounded annoyed when she said hello. Trevor was initially excited to talk with his father, but eventually became short and rude on the phone. Hearing his tone of voice, Susan became concerned that Trevor was shutting out his father. She reflected on what had happened and realized that her own behaviour and attitude was contributing to the problem. She started answering the phone right when it rang on the nights Trevor was scheduled to talk to his dad. Trevor's excitement about talking to his father soon returned.

2. Why does my 3-year-old child resist going to her father's? I know he is good to her.

There are many reasons why children resist going to the other parent's home even though they are emotionally close to them. Young children find it hard to leave one home to go to the other. Children are creatures of habit, and don't like changes. They like their own beds, toys, and familiar smells. They like routine, and like to stay put. Young children also experience 'separation anxiety' when they leave a parent. If they spend more time with one parent than the other, it is harder for them to leave that parent. When parents separate, children worry even more that they will lose their parents.

3. What can I do to encourage my 5-year-old's contact with her father?

There is plenty you can do to encourage access. First, keep the schedule firm, and allow no exceptions. Children thrive on routine. Arrange overnight access as soon as possible. Access that includes overnights shows longer-term success compared to more limited access (Maccoby & Mnookin, 1992).

To help younger children make the transition from one home to the other, create rituals. Prepare the younger child for visits by going over everything that will happen. Make it into a story, or even write it up into a book. Children are reassured by repetition because the repeated anticipation allows them to manage their fears. It provides them with words for the inner dialogue they need to help them overcome their fears.

For instance, you could say: 'Daddy will pick you up at 5 o'clock. I will answer the door, he'll come in. We'll get your suitcase, which will be ready on the dresser in your bedroom. You'll say goodbye to your room, your toys, and you'll take bunny. You'll put your red coat on, and I'll walk you to the car. There you'll say goodbye to me. Now you usually feel a little nervous and a little sad for a while in the car, but when you get to daddy's place, you usually settle down. Then you and daddy ...'

Let the child take a favourite toy with him. Tell him that you really want him to have a good time with his dad. Reassure him that he will not be missing anything at home. Tell him what you will be doing at home in his absence, stressing the usual routines (not anything he would hate to miss). Reassure him that you'll be here, waiting for him when he gets home. Let the child keep in touch with you by phone. Each home should have photos of the other parent, especially in the child's bedroom.

4. My 5-year-old son seems unclear about his desire to see his father. First he tells me that he does not want to go on visits. Then he wants to stay with his father all weekend, and yet when he gets home he says he did not have a good time. Help!

It is good that you are reflecting on what your son says instead of just reacting, or jumping to conclusions. Contradictory messages from children are hard to understand, yet they have their reasons. Why would your child say the above? First of all, the fact that children resent having to change from one home to another, and suffer separation anxiety, has already been mentioned. This may explain his difficulty leaving you – and leaving his father when he comes home. Then the fact that he tells you he did not have fun when he was with his father, even though you know he did, may be because he fears that when he is not with you, you are forgetting about him. And don't forget how children interpret things in a self-centred manner. Because your separation is recent, he is still worried about 'you leaving him, like his dad has,' and he wants to protect against that by making sure you know you are his favourite. Children try to protect themselves against further loss by saying what they think parents want to hear. Reassure your 5-year-old child that you both love him, and that you will not leave him, and that you are happy he is seeing his dad, who loves him.

5. **My ex and I are in constant conflict. After seeing her dad, my daughter tells me awful things about him. I'm sure they aren't true, but why does she say these things?**

Because you have a history of fighting, your daughter may feel caught between you and insecure about her place in your affections. Because you have separated in anger, your daughter thinks, 'If mom left dad when she was mad at him, will she leave me when she is mad at me?' Children look for ways to secure their place with both of you, and think that telling you negative things about the other parent will please you and make you love them more. It's as if they create a little triangle – 'You and me against someone you don't like.' They complain to each parent about the other as a way to stay close to both. Children do not say positive things about visits if they do not think positive reports will be welcomed.

6. **I don't know how my child can like my ex-husband, who is a very unpleasant person. I can't imagine that he gets much from visiting him.**

While difficult, it is important to separate your feelings about your ex from the feelings your child has about him. Your spouse may be unpleasant with you, and yet be very kind and appropriate with his son, whom he loves. It is almost like there are two people here: the husband you knew, and the separated father your child knows and *you do not know*. Sometimes there is little relationship between the two images. It is very important for you to hold on to this distinction, because children feel burdened and worried if you do not want them to spend time with the other parent. They will bend themselves out of shape to accommodate your wishes.

Children report how terrible they feel when their parents dislike and/or criticize each other. It's important to allow children their own opinion about the other parent. They need to be free of the pressure to please or take care of their parents.

7. What do I do when my child cries that she does not want to go home after our visits?

You reassure her. Children find transfers between homes difficult. Young children are distressed when separating from a parent, and they cry. Some parents worry that this shows something is wrong in the other parent's home. While this is a possibility, it is only one reason children cry. Another reason children cry on leaving a parent is related to that parent's feelings. Your child may be crying about leaving you because *you* may be sad about taking her back home. It is important to be aware of your own feelings, and to keep them separate from those of your children.

8. What do I say when my child says he wants us to get back together?

You say, 'No, we will not be getting back together. ' The child will probably be upset, and you will need to comfort her. It is normal for children to fantasize that you will reconcile. It is wishful or magical thinking, which you can look at as nature's way of letting children down gently. Children who are told clearly that there is no hope of reconciliation adjust better than those who nurture their fantasies.

9. It's impossible for me and my ex to be in the same room; too much has happened and we hate each other. When I think of him, negative emotions and memories overwhelm me. How do I handle this when the kids are talking about him and their visits?

You pretend. You learn to contain these feelings about the other parent. It can be done. Parents who feel hostile can act neutral and non-committal. They draw on different techniques to manage their hostilities. One father pretended he did not know the other parent and that she was his son's new parent. He practised treating her with the respect you would pay a new acquaintance. He was polite with her and was able to see her without the usual baggage.

If your child has witnessed fighting and mutual denigration

between you, have a talk with him. Tell him that you and your ex-partner are angry with each other. Explain that the anger is part of separating. Let him know that your anger does not stop him from loving and admiring his father. If you cannot make this kind of explanatory statement, it is better to say nothing. But the trouble with saying nothing is that it teaches your child that some things are off limits for discussion. This is not a message you want to send him, because it will make him alone with his thoughts and hurts, as well as create a growing rift between you.

10. **I am concerned about some of the statements my 8-year-old child makes when she returns from weekends about what my ex said about me.**

Children often blurt out what they see and hear: 'Dad says you're trying to make things difficult.' 'Daddy says you didn't pay up the car loan and now we have no car.' And they often misperceive and misunderstand. Because relations are tense, you must be careful not to overreact. Whatever your child says about you or her father, even if the information is totally wrong, do not jump in and correct it by telling your side of the story. *Say nothing about it. Do not justify yourself.* It will just increase the pressure on your child by putting her in the middle of a disagreement between you and her father. She will then not know who to believe and will worry about which of you is right. Children should not have to think about these things. They should be left out of your business. When your child tells you what the other parent said, respond with completely neutral statements: 'Oh is that so?' 'I see.' If you have gotten her caught between you, admit it and move on: 'I'm sorry you get stuck between mom and dad's problems, but we are trying to sort things out.' 'Being caught like this must be hard for you. We'll try to stop doing this.' 'Mom and dad are mad at each other, but it's not your fault.'

Many recently separated parents are easily upset when they hear anything about each other. Some speak negatively about each other to their child. This is unwise. Very unwise. You may justify it by telling yourself that the child should know what the other parent is really like. Do not fool yourself – by denigrating your ex you are pulling your child into an alliance with you against the other parent. You are creating a rift between your child and your ex that in the long term will also create a rift between you and your child. As children get older, they come to resent the badmouthing and the position it places them in. They learn eventually to distrust their parents. They may then vote with their feet.

11. **I know there is something wrong at my ex's. My 8-year-old son does not want to go to his father's home. I know kids should be with both parents, but should I force it?**

This is one of the toughest questions. Before you even think of restricting access, you need to be very sure there is a valid risk to your child. If you do think there is a child welfare issue, you need to alert a child protection authority. You will also probably require a clinical assessment.

Part III
Damage Control

12. When You Have to Go to Court and Clinical Assessments

For many parents there is both stress and relief associated with going to court. *Relief* because someone else – a judge – will finally make the decision for you, and because you will afterwards have less contact with your ex-partner. And *stress* because you will have little influence on the decision. It is important for you to know what the court process involves, how much it will cost, and how you can minimize your child's anguish as he watches his parents position themselves for a formal fight over him.

REASONS TO GO TO COURT

There are very few reasons to go to court after divorce. Most disputes about children and property can be resolved through the alternatives: dispute resolution processes, discussed in Chapter 8.

But in some situations, parents have profound worries about the other parent's ability to care for the children. If the behaviour of the other parent is putting your children at risk, you must report this to the child protection authorities. Going to court will help protect your children, but in the process it will probably increase the stress on your child and damage your relationship with the other parent. It is crucial that you minimize the side effects.

Concerns about the other parent's care can be categorized as follows:

1. The other parent has, in the past, neglected or abused a child.
2. The other parent has mental health problems.
3. The other parent is a substance abuser.
4. The other parent has a history of partner abuse.
5. The other parent is trying to alienate the child from his or her ex (parental alientation syndrome).

Where there are issues of physical safety:

- If physical conflict erupts between you and your ex-partner, you need to protect yourself and your children. CALL 911 for emergency assistance.
- If your physical safety is threatened, for immediate protection have on hand the phone numbers of emergency shelters.
- If you believe your children are at risk of physical or sexual abuse, act quickly and effectively.
- *Report your concerns to the local child protection authorities.* They will investigate and decide whether your situation warrants court action.

If You Think You Have a Child Protection Concern

1. Contact and remain connected to the child welfare authorities in your area.
2. Obtain the services of a child-focused lawyer. These lawyers are less interested in winning a case than in ensuring that children get what they need. Although lawyers talk about 'the child's best interests,' not all of them know how best interests translates into action that protects children. What is needed is a focus on the best possible plan for the child rather than a focus on parental allegations.
3. To see if yours concerns are valid, obtain a clinical assessment that is child focused.

In the past month, Darren had seen his 5-year-old daughter, Michelle, become sullen and withdrawn before and after time with her mother. One day after seeing a program on 'good touch, bad touch,' Michelle blurted out that she did not like her mother's boyfriend, Tom. Darren became alarmed and asked Michelle if Tom had ever touched her in a way she didn't like. For a long time, Michelle did not answer her father, but finally she divulged that she did not like Tom taking her to the washroom.

Alarmed, and suddenly worried that his daughter may have been sexually abused, Darren did not know whether to phone Michelle's mother or the child protection authorities. Because he was so worried, he decided to contact his local child welfare office and then his lawyer.

Parents who are trying to block each other's access to their children may allege all kinds of child abuse. In these situations, it is particularly important to obtain a clinical assessment in order to determine whether these safety issues are real or fabricated.

Shelly was outraged and hurt that her ex-partner, Cliff, had left her for another woman. She had heard that his new partner had a history of substance abuse. Shelly was frightened about her son's safety in the woman's presence. Moreover, she was unhappy about Cliff introducing her to their 8-year-old son, Danny. In the affidavits for court, she reported that Cliff's partner was a drug addict whose visits with Danny needed to be supervised. After an investigation by child protection authorities, several court appearances, and numerous cancelled visits between father and son, a clinical assessment revealed that Cliff's partner had been convicted of possession of marijuana seven years earlier, had undergone treatment, and was now drug free.

Damage Control: When You Have to Go to Court

1. When you are writing affidavits for court, do not exaggerate your allegations about your ex. These are public documents, and you want to make sure that if your children see them, now or in the future, they will not be hurt. Keep the language simple, and focus on your ex's *worrisome actions or behaviours* toward the child. Do not do a character assassination on your child's other parent.
2. Allow for amends. Make it clear that there are *specific behaviours*

that need to be *changed*, and that if they change, you will happily facilitate the best plan for the child.
3. Give the other parent a chance to correct the problem. The important thing is the safety of the child, not the exclusion of the other parent.
4. Give the professionals a chance. Check with them about the process of the assessment; do not have an agenda; be open to their feedback.
5. Do not tell the child the details of the court case.
6. Don't alienate the child from the other parent, regardless of the allegations.
7. Be sad, not mad. An attitude of regret is needed, not vengeance. You are taking this action to protect the child. If, after the problem is dealt with successfully, contact with the other parent is recommended, support it.
8. Never require a child to take the stand in court against a parent. Children will do it if they are asked, but it is extremely damaging to them.

CLINICAL ASSESSMENTS: WHAT TO EXPECT

In intractable disputes, lawyers, judges, and parents turn to assessments when they want to know what is best for a child. Because judges and lawyers are at arm's length from the family, and lack the clinical training and expertise to assess children's needs, it is hard for them to know exactly what the family needs. So they request or order an assessment from mental health experts who are neutral, clinically trained, and able to get close to the entire family. On the advice of their lawyers, parents agree to attend assessments.

Parents who get involved in an assessment are often not adequately prepared for its comprehensiveness and intrusiveness. Nor are they prepared for how long it can take. An assessment is conducted by a social worker, psychologist, or psychiatrist, and may take from six weeks to six months to complete. It is important that the same professional assess both parents and children. The more complex the situation and the greater the number of family members involved (grandparents, new partners), the longer and more expensive the process will be.

An assessment involves individual interviews with parents and children, as well as joint interviews with each parent with their children. Assessments may also include important extended family, such as grandparents, who increasingly are being recognized as making important contributions to the raising of children. The assessor collects information from parents, extended family, and the children. The assessor often conducts home visits with the family to get a truer picture of these relationships and a sense of the child's world. Community information (i.e., school reports, police records, medical reports, therapist reports) is a routine part of an assessment.

If the assessor sees an opportunity to mediate, or for parents to compromise, she may suggest this to them and encourage them to arrive at a settlement and avoid a trial. These are *mediative assessments*. Courts value assessments that resolve disputes, because conflict is damaging to children. If a resolution is not possible at the assessment stage, a report based on what was observed in the assessment is prepared. Its observations and recommendations are used by the lawyers and the judge to help parents settle at a case conference or a pretrial conference. If settlement is not possible, the report is presented as evidence in court.

The assessor prepares a written report for the court commenting on what was observed, the parenting abilities of each parent, their relationship with the children, and the needs of the children. Her recommendations are based on the best possible parenting arrangement for the children. Parents, lawyers, and the judge read the report; if the case proceeds to a trial, the assessor is usually called as a witness.

Assessments are helpful because they closely examine parenting concerns and abuse allegations. If you have concerns, it can be reassuring to know that the other parent has been carefully evaluated. You may worry that the assessor will be fooled, or taken in, by your ex-partner, who will be on his or her best behaviour. It is best to explain to the assessor your concerns and the reasons for them.

For parents, one of the most stressful things about a clinical assessment is the feeling they usually develop that the assessor is critical of them and is siding with the other parent. The assessor's job is to be neutral and to look only at the child's interests, which the separated parents often perceive differently. This is very threatening to the parents, and is one of the thorniest aspects of attending assessments: you would like the assessor to see things the way you see them, but that person needs to remain independent from both your perspectives in order to present that of the child's.

Parents express concern that the artificial atmosphere of the assessment will skew family relationships. Parents are stressed by assessments because they feel they are being scrutinized.

Assessments may be conducted by one person or by a clinical team. When several clinicians observe a situation – especially a very complicated one – a more accurate assessment can result. A thorough assessment can be more accurate than one based on only a few interviews. Some assessments focus on only one aspect of the family's functioning; these are brief. Lawyers will often suggest to you an assessor whose work they are familiar with. You can interview an assessor if you want to feel comfortable that your concerns will be understood.

Perhaps the worst part of being in an assessment is anticipating and then hearing the assessor's feedback, clinical opinions, and recommendations. Most assessors will comment on the positive and negative features of each caregiver's parenting style. But criticism, even if constructive, is painful to read or hear. Sometimes parents disregard anything that contradicts their own point of view. They become angry.

When you are given feedback, it is better to reflect on the criticism instead of dismissing anything that differs from you own perceptions. Think through the assessor's observations of your child's needs and thoughts about the cause of the dispute. Objective feedback about your family is important information. You are usually too close to your family to 'see the forest for the trees.' Around this time it is helpful to take an open attitude about the findings, and to explore the possibility of a settlement.

Jennifer was relieved when the assessor recommended that Greg improve his parenting skills, but was annoyed when the assessor talked about Jennifer's anger. The assessor told her that she thought Jennifer's anger with Greg was pushing 6-year-old, Crystal, away from him. Jennifer was upset. Since discovering his affair, Jennifer had been struggling to provide for Crystal. The assessor agreed that Jennifer had created a lovely home for Crystal. Jennifer cried and said how upset she was to have to put Jennifer through a divorce, especially since she herself came from a separated family.

WHAT IS IT LIKE TO GO TO COURT?

Many parents feel they must go to court to protect their children. They hope the judge will make a decision in their favour. But you may be surprised at the costs, in time and money, involved in settling a dispute in the courts. Each side files affidavits outlining its position, version of events, and concerns about the other. Reading these documents can feel very demeaning; allegations and accusations increase tension between parents. It is common for parents to point out and exaggerate each other's shortcomings in order to appear 'the better parent.' This is dangerous. Because the stakes are high, everything gets blown out of proportion. Things said in confidence appear in public documents. Family secrets are exposed. Trials are long, exhausting, and demeaning. You feel that the other parent has lied to undermine you. Attacked and humiliated, you feel pressured to settle for an unfair compromise. The alternative is to suffer through the trial process.

After Court Is Over

Because courts operate on a win/lose basis, most parents feel they have lost on some issues. You may have gone to trial only to end up with the arrangement that was suggested to you in the first place. In criminal trials, regardless of the outcome the parties do not have to see each other when the case is over. Whatever the allegations, they eventually fade into memory as time distances you from the experience. In family law, parents continue seeing each other, so whatever they say about each other in court will effect their relationship. That is why family court proceedings should stay civilized, and why parents need to pull their punches. When parents come away from court hurt and angry, the child's distress increases.

Recovering from a trial requires time, patience, and self-care. Trials have a greater impact than most people expect. You may feel humiliated that every facet of your life was exposed to scrutiny and discussion. You may feel angry that your ex distorted or lied to promote his or her case. You may feel that the system has bankrupted you financially and emotionally. If your contact with your children has been severely restricted or terminated as a result of the decision, you will need considerable help in dealing with this.

The good news is that court does come to an end. It is at this point that you must pick up your life and move on, without letting your grievances consume you. The intense feelings generated by court are often better managed in a safe, therapeutic environment. Keep those feelings away from the children. If your anger does not lessen over time, and interferes with your ability to resume your life or follow the orders of the court, find a therapist to help you to deal with your emotions. It is time to move on.

How Do Children Respond to Their Parents Going to Court?

Children are always distressed when you are fighting over them in court. Your fighting gives a lie to your reassurances to them that they are not the cause of your divorce. Like Ann said: 'How can I believe them when they say the divorce is not my fault when they are in court fighting over me?' When you go to court, your children feel forced to take sides, or feel terrified to express any opinion that might alienate you. Children are intimidated by the formal trappings of court. Court, to them, is associated with 'bad things.' Children often assume that they will have to speak to the judge in front of their parents. This rarely occurs, and parents who insist that their child should testify are subjecting their child to intolerable stress.

While you are preparing for court, your children often hear – or overhear – the details of the case. We have been amazed by what children know. They can read emotions and body language, and know exactly how their parents feel about each other. Often, they even know the allegations made. This is very wounding for a child.

Five-year-old Jack told us, 'Mommy got everything from the judge except us.' Nancy informed her mother, 'The judge will decide who is right, you or him.'

THE INVOLVEMENT OF OTHER PROFESSIONALS

Custody and access disputes can take months or years to resolve. During this time, parents often attend counselling for themselves or their children. This provides them with a safe place to air intense emotions. Because therapeutic relationships are based on trust, their confidentiality is very important. The role of the therapist in a custody dispute that goes to court is somewhat complicated. In situations like this, you may worry that your therapist will reveal the content of your therapy, or you may wish your therapist to say certain things in court to support your position. This is a delicate situation.

The court and assessors will review information from therapists that is relevant to the dispute. Relevant information might include how long the therapist has known the client, the reasons for involvement, the general issues that have been covered, and the progress the client has made. Unless the therapist has assessed *all* the adults and children in the dispute, an opinion regarding custody or visitation will not be given because such an opinion would be based on inadequate information.

In cases involving older children, a therapist may provide an account of the child's statements and wishes regarding the parenting plan. This can be tricky. It is important to hear and understand what children say; but at the same time, children caught in their parents' dispute often do not say what they mean. It is as if they are talking in code. It takes skill and expertise to tease out the exact meaning in their words. Sometimes a clear assessment of their wishes can only be made by observing their behaviour over time.

Assessments evaluate children both developmentally and in the context of family relationships. One-sided assessments can be inaccurate and biased. Most courts and professional bodies dismiss such assessments as frivolous and needlessly intrusive of the children.

13. Special Issues: Absent Parents, Spousal Assault, and Sexual Abuse Allegations

THE ABSENT PARENT RETURNS

The return of an absent parent is difficult and challenging for the child, the returning parent, and the residential parent. If well handled, a reunion can be a positive experience for the child. Children want to know their parents. And it is very important for them to talk to the returning parent about his or her absence, because children often blame themselves when a parent leaves.

There are many different reasons why parents leave. Some cannot tolerate the pain of the conflict and the feeling that their child is rejecting them. Others may have had addictions or criminal problems that interfered with their parenting. Still others may have left an abusive situation and were unable to take the children with them. For these parents, the wish to reconnect with their children can be intense and heartfelt. Yet it can threaten the residential parent and sometimes the child.

As the returning parent, you may be pretending to be more confident than you are. You may maintain your right to see your child, but emphasizing your rights may be a way of covering up your guilt for having left your child in the first place. You may feel anxious because you are anticipating the other parent's anger. It can be hard to admit why you left. Although your discomfort is understandable, do not react defensively or with bravado. These reactions can make the situation worse. It is better to be open and to admit your regret and remorse. Be prepared for the fact that you may or may not see your child. If you do see your child, she may take a long time to warm up to you. This is because children who have been abandoned have many layers of responses to work through.

As the residential parent, you will also experience many reactions to the other parent's return. You may have established a new life with new relationships. The return of the child's other parent can feel disruptive, intrusive, and threatening. Is he planning to stick around for just a little while, and then leave again, thus retraumatizing the child? Where has he been all these years while you struggled as a single parent? Why, when he was unable to behave responsibly in the past, does he have the right to return now simply because he feels some 'parental' connection? And finally, why should you have to deal with any of this, when even thinking about your ex brings back how rejected you felt when he left in the first place? These are some of the common reactions.

Is a Reintroduction of an Absent Parent in a Child's Best Interest?

If there are no safety or child protection concerns, and the parent appears to be committed, the answer is yes. Why? Because children whose parents leave them have scars to show for it. They take the abandonment personally. They think they are at fault, and feel rejected and devalued: 'Why would my father leave me unless there was something wrong with me?' 'I guess I'm not important enough for my father to take an interest in me. Maybe other people won't like me either.'

They also wonder, secretly, about the where and the why of that parent. It is important for children to hear that the parent left not because of something they did to drive him away, but because of the parents' problems or circumstances.

Guidelines for a Successful Reunion

If you undertake a reunion, take steps to give it a good chance of succeeding. A badly handled reunion is worse than no reunion. The child has already been traumatized once, and she should not be traumatized again. You must focus all your efforts on explaining the truth about the situation, while also protecting and supporting the child. The following are important guidelines for a successful reunion. To keep it simple, we refer to returning parents as fathers, which is not to deny that there are mothers who leave and later return to their children.

1. As the *residential parent*, you should be genuinely able to support the reunion. To that end, you must be able to process and deal with your own feelings and reactions to the return.
2. You must learn enough about the returning parent's reasons for leaving (and returning) to be certain that the reunion will be a good experience for the child. If the returning parent was violent in the past, you must be able to establish in your own mind that both you and your child will be physically and emotionally safe. If you have deliberately prevented your child from seeing her father in the past, you will need to own up to this with the child. A therapist can help you do this.
3. As the *returning parent*, you should be able to explain your reasons for leaving and your reasons for returning. Your explanation must be credible. And you must be clear in your commitment to consistent parenting now.
4. The child should have her own source of support, apart from her mother. She needs a neutral relationship in which she can deal with her own feelings safely, without worrying about hurting or disappointing. This person may be another family member, or a therapist with whom the child can develop a sense of safety and confidentiality.
5. The reunion should proceed slowly, in carefully controlled stages, facilitated by a clinician. The clinician meets first with the returning parent, then with the mother, and finally with the child. Only then do the family members meet. Here, also, there is a specific sequence to follow. First the mother and father meet, then the mother and child, and finally the father and child.

Steps to Managing a Successful Reunion

1. The Returning Parent

As the returning parent, you must understand that you hurt the child when you left. It is important for you to appreciate that the child experienced your absence as an abandonment of her, which is the worst crisis a child can endure. Thinking about this may be painful, but it will encourage you to be empathic to the child. You may then be more able to find ways to make it up to the child. You must also appreciate that the child, in your absence, has been solely dependent on her mother, who is now her anchor. It is very important that you not threaten this relationship. This is why it is crucial for you to reassure her mother about your motives and credibility. Understanding, and helping your child to understand, the reasons for your absence and for your return is very important. Was it something in yourself, or alienation or abuse by the residential parent, or rejection by the child? Or was it a combination of these factors?

2. The Residential Parent

Reunions succeed best when you, the residential parent, are confident that the returning parent poses no threat to you or the child or to the closeness between you. For that to happen, you need to be well engaged in the reunion process. Because of your pivotal position with the child, you need to be, in a sense, co-planning the reunion with the other parent. As you learn the reasons for his absence and for his return, you can encourage and reassure the child. Children are acutely sensitive to their parents' thoughts and wishes. If they sense that a visit will cause distress, they will deny their interest in the returning parent.

3. The Child

When a parent leaves, it is the child who is the wounded party, not the parents. It is the child who was left and hurt, and when the absent parent returns, it is the child who must be carefully surrounded with care and consideration. Only after the above steps have been taken, and are successful, does the process with the child begin.

First, the child's wishes are explored by the clinician. She needs to explore her feelings about having been left and about the return of the parent. She is encouraged to talk about her reactions to her father, and is reassured that her wishes will be respected. Many children are frightened or ambivalent about facing a returning parent. Because the returning parent left, they have little reason to trust that he will stay this time. They need to be allowed to take a 'wait and see' approach; after all, the reunion may not work. Under no circumstances should the child feel pressured to see or not see her father.

4. The Parents Together

Before the returning parent meets with the child, the parents meet to discuss certain issues with the assessor. The parents should update each other about their current lives and explore each other's intentions for the child. After the parents reach some commitment to cooperate for the child's sake, a *slow* process begins in which the child gets to know the returning parent.

5. The Child and the Residential Parent

The residential parent needs to give the child permission to see the returning parent and to be with him. Parents sometimes struggle to find the right words, and a joint session with the child and the assessor can be helpful. In advance of this, both parents need to agree on what they will say to the child to prepare her for the first visit. Blaming statements must be avoided because they put the child in a loyalty bind. Questions about *why* the parent was absent should be left to the returning parent to answer.

6. The Visit

The parents are usually worried about the reunion, and should work with an assessor or therapist to manage their discomfort and distress. For the first while, the assessor stays in the room with the child and the returning parent. When they are comfortable, and the reunion is progressing well, it is helpful for the mother to watch from behind a one-way mirror. This is often reassuring and informative.

The assessor stays with the mother as she watches, to provide whatever support is necessary.

Don was struggling with a serious addiction problem when he disappeared from Helen and their 2-year-old son, Dylan. Four years later, after being drug-free for one year, he contacted Helen, who refused to see him. After involving lawyers, the parents agreed to meet with an assessor, who assessed the potential for reintroduction. Initial meetings were highly charged: Helen, now living with a new partner and the mother of a 6-month-old baby, was outraged at Don's return. Don tried to reassure Helen that he had 'cleaned up his act.' He told her he was sorry he had abandoned her and Dylan and that he wanted to make up for the past. Helen just wanted to take Dylan and run, she was frightened of being hurt again – it had taken so long to recover before. She softened when she thought about how often Dylan asked after his own father now that his stepsister had hers. Although it was hard for her, Helen eventually put aside her own doubts and reservations to facilitate a reintroduction of Dylan to his father.

Dylan, aware of his mother's distress, was at first reluctant to see his father. His mother gave him permission to see his dad, reassuring him that she would be all right and that the therapist would supervise. Don brought games and a snack, and planned a low-key visit. As father and son became more comfortable, Don told Dylan he was sorry for having left him and for having been away so long. Dylan asked his father why he was away and where he had been. Don explained that he had serious personal problems and needed to get help before returning. He added that his problems had never been Dylan's fault, and that although he had been away a long time, he wanted Dylan to know he had never forgotten about his son. He then explored with Dylan how he felt about his return.

The timing of the process must be at the child's pace.

Seven-year-old Tommy suggested that he wanted physical distance from his father: 'I don't want him to get too close to me.' When his father was informed of this, he and the assessor came up with the idea of showing Tommy photos of himself and his father from earlier times. While looking at the photos, Tommy's father accidentally touched his arm. Tommy shrank back, shouting, 'Don't touch me, I hate you.' His father apologized for touching him and looked at him gently. Tommy burst into tears and told his father he had been a 'bad dad.'

SPOUSAL ASSAULT AND ACCESS

In the past decade, we have become more aware of family violence and the damage it does to families and children. In a summary of the research in this area, Peter Jaffe, David Wolfe, and Susan Wilson (1990) stated that one in ten women are abused every year by the man with whom they live. In 55 per cent of these households there are two or more children, and 30 to 40 per cent of these children may also be victims of abuse. Most of these children will *witness* conflict and violence between their parents, and this has profoundly negative effects on their emotional and psychological development. Children growing up in an atmosphere of fear and anxiety brace themselves for the next violent incident. Some children develop a sense of responsibility for preventing further abuse from happening. Children in violent homes learn that violence is a method of resolving conflicts. They also feel ashamed of the violence and try to conceal it. This isolates them and makes it hard for them to confide in people outside the family.

Most often, it is the woman who leaves her violent partner, in an attempt to escape crippling fear and a life of emotional and physical violence. A history of spousal violence creates a complicated situation for the separating family.

When children have witnessed violence between their parents, and the aggressive parent will not change, it serves no useful purpose for the child to have visits with him. When children are terrified of a violent parent, the emotional stress created by the visits undermines their emotional well-being as well as that of the residential parent. Moreover, in these situations, visits are sometimes used as an excuse for the nonresidential parent to stalk and harass the victimized parent.

Violence in any form is devastating and damaging to children and to victimized parents, and children always need to be protected from it. The difficulty is that in some cases of spousal abuse, it is unclear exactly what happened in the relationship. Parents give conflicting reports of the same events, and there are few if any third-party reports. Also difficult are situations where the children continue to feel close to both parents.

How are separated families best helped in these situations? These cases first require an assessment of the context, extent, and severity of the violence. Research has isolated different types of violence between separating couples. It is important to be clear on the cause of the abuse when determining the best parental plan.

Different Situations Call for Different Solutions

Johnston and Campbell (1993) studied couples with a history of spousal violence, and outlined four different types of spousal violence:

1. Men with a low tolerance for frustration who use violence as a way to control and terrorize the women on whom they are highly dependent.
2. Women who become angry and violent toward their partner when gripped by their own intense anxieties and frustrations.
3. Men and women whose disagreements escalate into mutual physical violence. Although mutual at first, the man eventually overpowers the woman because of his superior physical strength.
4. Separation and post-divorce violence, which occur as a reaction to traumatic separation or stressful litigation. In these cases, violence did not occur during the relationship – it was induced by the divorce.

Spousal violence is always an alarming factor that must be evaluated carefully when post-separation plans for children are being established. However, not all cases of violence are the same. A husband who loses control and becomes violent on discovering that his wife has left without warning, is not the same as a husband who abuses alcohol, assaults his wife routinely, and denies responsibility for his abuse.

If violence was, or is, a parent's characteristic way of handling stress and problems, and the parent denies this pattern, unsupervised access is clearly not appropriate. When a father is unable to control his emotions and physical reactions to a child, the benefits of supervised access are questionable. When a father persists in violence, there are consequences to him as a parent. The focus here is on protecting the child, not the rights of the parent.

A child who has been traumatized by witnessing violence in her parent cannot attend visits ignoring that fact. On the other hand, if she is able to use the visits to address her parent's abusive behaviour, this greatly benefits her. This will only happen if the offending parent has taken responsibility for the violent behaviour. When a father who has abused his wife will not take responsiblity for the abuse and discuss it with the child who witnessed it, the child has to pretend the abuse did not happen. This is hurtful to the child. It is emotionally abusive for a child to have to pretend that the violence she witnessed did not occur.

On the other hand, if a father is genuinely sorry for abusing his partner, and attends counselling to confront his behaviour, and deals with those patterns in a constructive way, it may be possible over time to move to unsupervised visits, with only the transfers of the children being monitored to protect the mother from further stress. For this to be successful, the abusing parent needs to be able to reassure the other parent and the children that he is taking effective steps to address his problems. He needs to accept responsibility for his past behaviour and make appropriate amends. Visits must flow out of genuine interest in the children, not a desire for contact with the ex-partner. The child must be the focus. If the abusing parent questions the children about their mother, or uses transfers to contact her, the benefits of visits are highly questionable.

Tasks of the Parents

If you have been physically abused by your ex-partner, and your ex wishes to see the children, you and your family may benefit from a comprehensive clinical assessment. Because abuse is a disorganizing and traumatizing experience, women need counselling to resolve this trauma, so that its effects do not become embedded in their daily lives.

If you have a history of abusing your spouse, it is critical for you to seek out counselling and/or treatment for your inability to control your anger. Spousal abuse is a serious sociological and psychological problem that requires many levels of intervention. Many fathers, out of denial or misplaced embarrassment, minimize the impact of their violent behaviour. This can lead to further abuse.

Post-separation arrangements in these situations have to ensure the safety of the mother and children. If you have abused your spouse, you will have to tolerate restrictions and limitations. Unless you confront your behaviour and change it, you run the risk of undermining and permanently rupturing your relationship with your children. Some fathers successfully confront the reasons for their use of violence to deal with life's problems, and develop more adaptive strategies. Others are unwilling or unable to confront their own histories and behaviours, and continue to pursue their ex-spouses. Eventually they alienate their children entirely.

SEXUAL ABUSE ALLEGATIONS IN CUSTODY AND VISITATION DISPUTES

In the last ten to fifteen years in North America, with more children and adults coming forward with disclosures, the sexual abuse of children has become an important social issue. Treatment and prevention programs have been developed to support children who have been victimized; schools and mental health agencies have created child streetproofing programs; and parents have become more vigilant about their children's safety.

The abuse of children is a criminal offence in our society, and all allegations require investigation. Allegations of abuse result in the involvement of the child protection and criminal systems. When a child or adult alleges child sexual abuse, child protection authorities respond within twenty-four hours. The police are called to interview the alleged victim and the offender. This difficult situation needs to be handled with skill and sensitivity so that children are not hurt by the investigation and by the stress of possible court action. When children are hurt, or 'revictimized' by the services designed to help them, they suffer yet another crisis.

The Controversy about False Allegations

There is great controversy about sexual abuse allegations that arise during custody and access disputes. It has been thought that these allegations are rampant in custody and access disputes, and that these allegations are usually false. It has also been suggested that vindictive and falsely accusing mothers make these allegations against fathers to exclude them from access. These are damaging myths that lead parents and professionals to give reduced importance to sexual abuse allegations arising in custody and access disputes.

The Truth about Sexual Abuse Allegations in Disputes

(If you are not interested in statistics, skip this section and move on to the next.)

The statistics in this area remain confusing and contradictory. The findings in many studies contradict each other and there are numerous problems with sample sizes and methodology. We cite findings from only those studies that have the largest sample size and the soundest methodology.

In 1990, Thoennes and Tjaden studies 9,000 families contesting custody and access disputes throughout eight different court jurisdictions in the United States. Only 2 per cent of these cases involved sexual abuse allegations. This is a greater number of allegations than found in the general population.

After being investigated, 33 per cent of these allegations were considered false, 50 per cent were seen to be probable and 17 per cent were indeterminate (this is as judged by professionals, not as determined by the justice system).

To help you make sense of this, you need to know that 6 to 8 per cent of the sexual abuse allegations brought forward in the general population are considered false. Although this shows that false allegations are more likely in custody disputes, the number of false allegations does not constitute the epidemic that the media has suggested, or the elevated figures earlier researchers have found (Green, 1986; Benedek & Schetky, 1985). Important also to note is that although the number of false allegations is greater in custody disputes, 50 per cent of these allegations are probable. This is approximately the same ratio of probability that is found in the general population (Jones & McGraw, 1987).

In summary, while there appears to be a higher proportion of false allegations in contested divorce cases, the proportion that are likely true remains very high. This suggests that these cases require the same careful investigation as all others to ensure the safety of the children involved.

A Bomb Goes Off in the Family

Allegations of sexual abuse arising in family situations are very serious and disturbing. So are allegations that arise during and after separation and divorce. When a family is going through a custody/access dispute, sexual abuse allegations make a complicated situation a hundred times more difficult. For the child, the stakes are very high.

The tension and antagonism of custody and access disputes provides fertile ground for these allegations to come forward (Faller, 1991). There are reasons why *true allegations* are made at this time. A child disclosing that she was abused may be the cause of the separation. Or the child may start talking about her sexual abuse only because the parent who abused her has moved out. A parent may sexually abuse a child during the stressful process of separating. Or a parent may approach a child sexually because the other parent is not there to supervise.

There are also reasons why *false allegations* may arise during custody/access disputes. Sometimes one parent wants to exclude the other parent from the child's life (see Chapter 10). Alleging sexual abuse is a powerful tool for accomplishing this. Moreover, because some disputing parents hold excessively negative views of each other, they expect the worst. They worry too much about their children being hurt by the other parent, and can overreact to things.

A 4-year-old was fussy before and after visits. She also developed redness in her genital area. Her mother, stressed by the separation and worried about her husband's past destructiveness, put these two things together and thought they indicated sexual abuse.

False allegations can also arise when a parent with a history of childhood sexual abuse is overly vigilant to signs of sexual abuse, and too sensitive to general physical contact (such as hugging) between the other parent and the child. This heightened vigilance colours her perception of the father–child relationship. It is very important to note that most false allegations in divorce and custody disputes are *not* the result of deliberate falsifications (Guyer & Ash, 1986, as cited in Wakefield & Underwager, 1991).

Why Is It All So Confusing?

In the past ten years there have been contradictory statistics regarding the number of sexual abuse allegations arising in custody and access disputes. The media have reported that there is an epidemic of false allegations.

Moreover, it is often very difficult to determine whether the allegations in these disputes are true or false. It would seem that some sexual abuse allegations are based on misunderstandings, or possibly one parent is fabricating the abuse in order to shut the other parent out. But the assumption that all allegations are false is clearly a dangerous approach. Another common misconception is that allegations of sexual abuse are made mainly by mothers against fathers. More and more fathers are making allegations of sexual abuse by mothers, or by mothers' partners who are in contact with the children (Elterman & Ehrenberg, 1991).

How to Proceed When Allegations Exist

All sexual abuse allegations need to be taken seriously, including those in custody and access disputes. For separated families, these allegations are best handled with a clinical assessment. Assessments consider the outcome of child protection investigations, and try to determine the best plan for the children. When an allegation arises during the assessment itself, it has the effect of a bomb going off in the family. It has the power to stop access and derail the assessment. In these situations, the assessment is put on hold until child protection authorities complete their investigation of the case.

Allegations of sexual abuse always require the intervention of child protection authorities. They are a clear indication that a child is in need of protection. If the allegation is *true*, the child needs protection from the abusive parent. If the allegation is *false*, the child may need protection from the parent who is misconstruing, misunderstanding, or falsely accusing. If the abuse can be neither substantiated nor ruled out, the case returns to the assessment process. Assessing disputes involving allegations, especially unsubstantiated ones, is like doing brain surgery with boxing gloves on.

Michelle and Sam were married for three years before separating. Their separation was 'a nightmare' by both accounts, and their communication since had been sparse and hostile. Four-year-old Mark lived with his mother and visited his father every second weekend. Mark returned home from these visits telling his mother he was sleeping with his daddy 'without pyjamas.' She also noted an increased amount of physical contact between them at transfers. She worried about Mark's crying when he came home. She had a vague memory that when Mark was a baby, her husband had played with his penis when he was changing his diapers. Over time, Michelle became worried that Sam was sexually abusing their son, even though Mark did not say so. Nevertheless, on the strength of her credibility, and because of the nature of her worries, visits were stopped, and then supervised for a period of months.

When the family was referred for an assessment, Sam expressed shock about Michelle's sexual abuse allegations. He could not understand her concerns about his sharing a bed with Mark. On exploring his experience, Sam described growing up in the Far East, where it was commonplace for families to sleep in the same room. He talked about sharing a bed with his siblings, in the same room as their parents. They all wore underwear and thought nothing of being naked. To Sam, his sleeping arrangements with his son were a continuation of his earlier habits.

Michelle was encouraged to discuss her worries in detail. She described what she felt was an 'overly close' relationship between Sam and his son. She was uncomfortable with the amount of physical contact between them. When discussing her background, she explored the emotional coldness in her family. She noted there was no expression of affection between members of her family. From behind the one-way mirror, she showed the assessor what she considered examples of inappropriate closeness in the father–son play. She was helped to differentiate what was normal from what seemed to be her fears. Where Sam was overly close, we provided direction about appropriate boundaries. Sam was directed to arrange for Mark to sleep in his own bed, and father and son donned pyjamas. Much later in the assessment, she disclosed incidents of sexual interference by her father.

Both parents became more sensitive to each other's issues and to Mark's needs. Michelle sought out therapy to deal with her childhood trauma. Sam attended parent education.

In another family, a clinical assessment empowered a mother who worried that her husband was sexually abusing their daughter, to take her worries seriously. She was encouraged to contact the child welfare authorities. To them, she explained the history and nature of her worries. They interviewed her daughter and her husband. The child welfare agency validated her concerns, and visits with the father were terminated.

When Abuse Can't Be Substantiated

Because some sexual abuse allegations are hard to prove or validate, it is sometimes not clear what, if anything, may have happened to the child. These situations can be very difficult for the child, and frustrating and anxiety provoking for both parents. What little trust and good will may have existed between the parents is usually completely exhausted by the end of the investigation.

To protect children who have already been through the ordeal of an investigation, it is best to proceed slowly and with caution.

In the absence of substantiation, parents still have to make sense of their experiences, and life for the child must somehow continue. Parents need help to understand how and why the allegations arose, and help to manage their fear and anger about what happened. Children need to be reassured that they will be protected. They need to be educated, or 'streetproofed,' so that they will report inappropriate touching whether outside or within the family.

Starting with supervised visits can be reassuring to everyone. The children feel protected, the accused parent is protected by the knowledge that a third party will report what happens during visits, and the alleging parent knows the child is safe. Over time, if visits go well, unsupervised contact can be restored.

SUPERVISED ACCESS

Supervised access involves visits monitored or supervised by a third party, who may be a realtive or a professional. Usually, supervised visits are arranged when there is concern about the child's safety in the presence of the visiting parent. The third party ensures that the child is safe and reports back to the parent with the concern, and to lawyers and assessors.

Attending supervised visits can be awkward, particularly if you have not seen your children for a long time. You are not sure what to say, or how to explain, or how to plan the visit. It is important to plan the visit carefully, and to include time for connecting, playing, explaining, and forecasting.

After supervised visits were ordered because of his drinking problem, John knew he would feel uncomfortable and upset when he first saw his children, aged 9 & 7. What would he say to Monica and Eric? What would they ask him? Should he tell them he had been struggling with an alcohol problem? John decided to first talk only about neutral topics related to the children, such as school and hobbies. He brought a snack and pictures of where he now lived and worked. In case it came up, he prepared an honest explanation for why the visits were now supervised and rehearsed telling the chil-

dren that this change was not their fault. He also knew and could tell them how often he would be seeing them and gave the children a copy of the schedule of visits.

When the children were asked about the first visit with their father, Eric said he liked the snack because 'it made me feel less scared.' He was relieved when his father took the lead and asked 'about the easy stuff.' Both children were surprised when he told them about his drinking problem. 'We couldn't believe it when he said that stuff,' said Monica.

Some residential parents are at a loss how to explain supervised visits to children. They do not want to say negative things about the supervised parent, yet they want to alert their children to the other parent's potential to harm them. Sometimes they feel they have to say negative things to protect the children from possible harm: 'If I don't warn him that his father is a shiftless person, if he doesn't follow through, the kids will just be hurt again.' Because children are safe in a supervised setting, it is best to say less rather than burden children with complicated and involved explanations. You just have to say, 'You'll visit with mom [or dad] in a safe place where there will be other parents and kids who are also visiting. This way, there won't be any problems and everyone can have a good time.'

Tips on How to Use Supervised Visits

1. Contain your Negative Feelings toward the Other Parent

Be neutral and calm about these visits, because your children will notice any anxiety you have and they will be upset. Containing your anxiety is difficult, so you need to plan strategies to help you handle your feelings. One mother used 'deep breathing' techniques when she realized that her shallow breathing made her more tense: 'I was so nervous, I was panting.' A father who had not seen his child for three months was so upset at the time lost that he wanted to scream at his ex. Instead, he used visualization: instead of seeing his wife as someone who had deprived him of their son, he focused on how connected his son was to her and treated her like the special person she was to his son. He discovered that when he treated his ex well, he liked her better. Another mother wrote angry letters to her ex, but did not send them. Over time, some of her anger dissipated and she was able to face the visits with him more calmly.

2. Take Your Time and Approach the Visit Slowly

Much as you, the visiting parent, would like to develop a close relationship with your child as quickly as possible, you would be wise to let your child set the pace. Children are often shy, anxious, and hesitant about seeing a parent after a long time. Unless your child initiates physical contact, it is best to greet him gently. Allow him to establish a comfortable distance from you. Some children immediately approach their parents, while others are more hesitant. Take an interest in whatever activity he chooses, and allow him to invite you to play. Children are usually comfortable answering questions about school, their friends, and so on, but will often clam up if questioned about the family, the other parent, or personal feelings. They do not want to say anything that may cause an argument.

3. Length of Time in Supervised Access

Parents usually agree to supervised visits when they are a temporary measure. Conflict arises when the residential parent wants them extended. Nonresidential parents usually hope to graduate to unsupervised access as soon as possible. Some residential parents eventually feel reassured about the other parent's reliability, and become comfortable over time with a less restricted arrangement. Other residential parents cannot agree to unsupervised access even when the other parent seems reliable and focused on the child's needs. Some situations require a full assessment and recommendations from a professional.

Some parents function better with their children in supervised access because it provides a structure that they themselves cannot provide. If possible, these parents should continue indefinitely in supervised access.

Fred lived an unstructured lifestyle as a travelling salesman. His ex-wife,

Monica, was concerned that he 'lived in a suitcase' and that he had no suitable home for visits with 3-year-old Sally. When Sally and her father had visits at the parent–child centre, Fred learned a whole new way of being with Sally. They enjoyed the playground, toys, snack time, and library area. The staff at the centre helped Fred with his child-rearing skills and taught him how to make crafts with Sally. Sally was more relaxed after visits, which raised Sally's mother's confidence. In this situation the whole family agreed to continue using the centre for visits.

In some situations, a parent's behaviour may be damaging to a child. He or she may be unable to acknowledge or change those behaviours, in which case even supervised contact is questionable. The courts often protect children by ordering no contact with such a parent. These cases require careful investigation and assessment before any final decision is made.

Conclusion

Perhaps people enter into marriage and parenthood a little too quickly and with not quite enough thought. In Britain in the 1980s, concern about rising divorce rates and their social consequences resulted in the development of state-financed programs to support marriage. Therapeutic interventions were offered at the most crucial points in marriage: the premarriage period, the time of the first child, and the 'empty-nest' stage, when children leave home.

Perhaps we need to rethink our traditional (authoritarian) model of family life, which persists to this day. We need to actively encourage a more egalitarian model – one that involves both parents in child rearing. We need to re-emphasize the importance of the extended family. To involve parents more equally in their children's upbringing, we will have to rethink how workplaces are organized. This may lead to job sharing, a shorter work week, on-site child care, and greater scope for paternity leave.

These, however, are the longer-term solutions. For the time being, what can we do to alleviate the plight of children who are forced to adjust to conditions that are not always optimal to their well-being? When families separate, all possible effort must be made to keep *both parents* meaningfully connected to their children. The question is not *which* parent should care for the children, but how *both* parents will care for their children.

This book has offered you an opportunity to reflect on how to achieve a good divorce and avoid the damage of a highly conflicted one. The patterns you create after separation often determine how

things will go in the future. Yet immediately after separation is probably the hardest time to co-operate, given the amount of pain and
anger you are experiencing. There are several roads open before you,
each with a very different destination. The best road, of course, is the
amicable or disengaged one. These kinds of separations allow children the best chance of recuperating from their losses. The one road
you definitely want to avoid is the conflicted divorce. The 'divorce
from hell' damages children and families for long periods of time.

Travellers en route to the good divorce grieve their losses, painful
as they are. They feel their pain but do not pass it on to their children
or ex-spouses. Those on the road to the divorce from hell do not feel
pain – they only feel anger and resentment. It is everyone *around*
them who carries their pain – especially their children.

Family disruption is painful and full of emotional traps. Recovering from it can become a journey of self-discovery and self-care –
a second chance for parents and children both. But that second
chance only comes if you resolve, or at least manage, your spousal
conflict, stay focused on your children, and honour a rich and well-
developed parenting plan. Your plan has to encourage a meaningful parenting role for both of you in your child's life.

Let bygones be bygones. Your relationship with your children and
your efforts at healing yourself are the only things over which you
have control. As you and your children grieve, and learn to master
the difficult tasks of divorce, you all will live well because of your
efforts.

Appendix

Finding Therapeutic Resources

Here are some of the ways to find therapeutic resources for you and your children.

1. The fastest way to accumulate a list of resources is to ask several key people or agencies for information. Contact your family doctor, or your local children's mental health agency or social service agency. Your lawyer may be aware of specialists in the field of separation and divorce. Be sure and ask if there is a fee attached to the service.
2. Indicate that you are looking for the names of individuals or programs specializing in or knowledgeable about your type of situation.
3. Contact the resources you find and ask them about their training and expertise. Approach this initial interviewing process as an important part of getting connected with the right person or service.
4. Be prepared to make a time commitment.

Individual therapists should be able to tell you how they work (the model they use, and whether their work is time-limited or long-term, and so on), but they will likely need to do an assessment before they can tell you exactly what type of treatment plan makes sense.

Group programs for adults and children usually have a specific focus and content so that you have a good idea of exactly what gets covered.

Divorce Support Services in Toronto

ALTERNATIVES:
Phone: (416) 223-7113.

AMEND (A Method for Ending Negative Divorce).
Phone: (416) 408-1919.

COPING WITH SEPARATION.
Phone: (519) 941-9379 or (888) 424-7464.

DADS CANADA INC. (Divorce and Defence Strategies).
Phone: (416) 232-9025.

DIVORCE & SEPARATION SEMINARS. Sponsored by Separated Anonymous.
Phone: (416) 283-3305.

FAMILIES IN TRANSITION.
Phone: (416) 585-9151

THE FAMILY LAW INSURANCE CENTRE.
Phone: (800) 529-4333 or (416) 620-1660.

'FOR KIDS' SAKE' PROGRAM.
A group/research/treatment program for high and medium conflict post-divorce families at the Centre for Addiction and Mental Health, Clarke Division. Children attend ten weeks of therapy in peer groups; over the same time, their parents attend the parents' program. Parents are seen separately in peer groups for five weeks and then together in a larger group for five weeks. In the separated groups, parents are taught new ways of understanding the conflict they are facing and its impact on their particular child. Then, in the larger group, they are encouraged to develop new, improved parental plans. In developing these plans, they are assisted by the children's therapists, who offer suggestions about each child's needs. Phone: (416) 979-4954.

HEART (Human Equality Action and Resource Team).
Phone: (416) 410-4141.

JEWISH FAMILY AND CHILD SERVICE.
Phone: (905) 882-2331 or (416) 638-7800.

KIDS HELP PHONE.
Phone: (800) 668-6868.

NEW BEGINNINGS.
Phone: (416) 222-1101, ext. 107 or 258.

NEW DIRECTIONS.
Phone: (416) 487-5317

PARENTS WITHOUT PARTNERS.
Phone: (416) 925-2045 or (416) 466-5588.

PEEL COUNSELING AND CONSULTING SERVICES.
Phone: (905) 567-8858 or fax (905) 567-6559.

SELF-HELP RESOURCE CENTRE OF GREATER TORONTO.
Phone: (416) 487-4355.

TORONTO FATHERS' RESOURCES.
24–hour hotline: (416) 861-0626.

A WEEKEND FOR SINGLES.
Phone: (416) 480-2291 or (416) 663-8491.

References

Adler, R. (1988). *Sharing the Children: How to Resolve Custody Problems and Get On with Your Life*. Bethesda, MD: Adler & Adler.

Ahrons, C.R. (1994). *The Good Divorce: Keeping Your Family Together When Your Marriage Comes Apart*. New York: HarperCollins.

Amato, P.R., and B. Keith (1991). Parental divorce and the well-being of children: A meta-analysis. *Psychological Bulletin*, 110(1): 26–46.

Benedek, E.P., and D.H. Schetky (1985). Allegations of sexual abuse in child custody and visitation disputes. In D.H. Schetky and E.P. Benedek (eds.), *Emerging Issues in Child Psychiatry and the Law*, 145–56. New York: Brunner/Mazel.

Bisnaire, L.M., P. Firestone, and D. Rynard (1990). Factors associated with academic achievement in children following parental separation. *American Journal of Orthopsychiatry*, 60(1): 67–76.

Bohannan, P. (1970). The six stations of divorce. In P. Bohannan (ed.), *Divorce and After*. Garden City, N.Y.: Doubleday and Co.

Bowlby, J. (1982). Attachment and loss: Retrospect and prospect. *American Journal of Orthopsychiatry*, 52(4): 664–78.

– (1980). *Attachment and Loss*. Vol. 3, *Loss, Sadness and Depression*. New York: Basic Books.

Braver, S.H., S.A. Wolchik, I.N. Sandler, B. Fogas, and D. Zvetina (1991). Frequency of visitation by divorced fathers: Differences in reports by fathers and mothers. *American Journal of Orthopsychiatry*, 61(3): 448–54.

Brown, L.K., and M. Brown (1986). *Dinosaurs' Divorce: A Guide for Changing Families*. Boston: The Atlantic Monthly Press.

Buchanan, C.M., E.E. Maccoby, and S.M. Dornbusch (1991). Caught between parents: Adolescents' experience in divorced homes. *Child Development*, 62(5): 1008–29.

Camara, K.A., and G. Resnick (1989). Styles of conflict resolution and cooperation between divorced parents: Effects on child behavior and adjustment. *American Journal of Orthopsychiatry*, 59(4): 560–75.

Cherlin, A.J. (1981). *Marriage, Divorce, Remarriage*. Cambridge, MA: Harvard University Press.

Dennis, W. (1996). The divorce from hell. *Toronto Life*, February.

Department of Justice (1997). *Federal Child Support Guidelines: A Guide to the New Approach*. Ottawa: Communications and Executive Services Branch.

Elliott, J., and M. Richards (1991). Children and divorce: Educational performance and behavior before and after parental separation. Unpublished manuscript as cited in Kelly (1993).

Elterman, M.F., and M.F. Ehrenberg (1991). Sexual abuse allegations in child custody disputes. *International Journal of Law and Psychiatry*, 14: 269–86.

Faller, K.C. (1991). Possible explanations for child sexual abuse allegations in divorce. *American Journal of Orthopsychiatry*, 61 (1), 86–91.

Furstenberg, F.F. Jr., and A.J. Cherlin (1991). *Divided Families: What Happens to Children When Parents Part*. Cambridge: MA: Harvard University Press.

Gardner, R.A. (1992). *The Parental Alienation Syndrome: A Guide for Mental Health and Legal Professionals*. Cresskill, NJ: Creative Therapeutics.

Garrity, C.B., and M.A. Baris (1994). *Caught in the Middle: Protecting the Children of High-Conflct Divorce*. New York: Lexington Books.

Green, A.H. (1986). True and false allegations of sexual abuse in child custody disputes. *Journal of the American Academy of Child Psychiatry*, 25(4): 449–56.

Greif, J.B. (1979). Fathers, children and joint custody. *American Journal of Orthopsychiatry*, 49(2): 311–19.

Guidubaldi, J., and J.D. Perry (1985). Divorce and mental health sequelae for children: A two-year follow-up of a nationwide sample. *Journal of the American Academy of Child Psychiatry*, 24(5): 531–7.

Guyer, M., and P. Ash (1986). Child abuse allegations in the context of adversarial divorce. Paper presented at the Annual Meeting of the American Academy of Psychiatry and the Law, Los Angeles, as cited in H. Wakefield, and R. Underwager (1991).

Hess, R.D., and K.A. Camara (1979). Post-divorce family relationships as mediating factors in the consequences of divorce for children. *Journal of Social Issues*, 35(4): 79–96.

Hetherington, E.M. (1989). Coping with family transitions: Winners, losers, and survivors. *Child Development*, 60(1): 1–14.

Hetherington, E.M., M. Cox, and R. Cox (1985). Long-term effects of divorce and remarriage on the adjustment of children. *Journal of the American Academy of Child Psychiatry*, 24(5): 518–30.

– (1982). Effects of divorce on parents and children. In M.E. Lamb (ed.), *Nontra-*

ditional Families: Parenting and Child Development, 233–88. Hillsdale, NJ: Lawrence Erlbaum Associates.

- (1981). Children and divorce. In R.W. Henderson (ed.), *Parent-Child Interaction: Theory, Research and Prospects*. 33–58. New York: Academic Press.
- (1978). The aftermath of divorce. In J.H. Steven and M. Matthews (eds.), *Mother/Child, Father/Child Relationships*, 149–76. Washington, DC: National Association for the Education of Young Children.

Hodges, W.F. (1986). *Interventions for Children of Divorce: Custody, Access and Psychotherapy*. New York: John Wiley and Sons.

Hodges, W., R. Wechsler, and C. Ballantine (1979). Divorce and the preschool child: Cumulative stress. *Journal of Divorce*, 3(1): 755–67. As cited in Amato and Keith (1991).

Holmes, T.H., and R.H. Rahe (1967 [1991]). The social readjustment rating scale. *Journal of Psychosomatic Research*. 11: 213–18.

Jaffe, P., D. Wolfe, and S. Wilson (1990). *Children of Battered Women*. Newbury Park, CA: Sage Publications.

Johnston, J.R. (1993). Children of divorce who refuse visitation. In C. Depner and J.H. Bray (eds.), *Non-Residential Parenting: New Vistas in Family Living*, 109–35. Newbury Park, CA: Sage Publications.

Johnston, J.R., and L.E.G. Campbell (1993). A clinical typology of interparental violence in disputed-custody divorces. *American Journal of Orthopsychiatry*, 63(2): 189–99.

- (1988). *Impasses of Divorce: The Dynamics and Resolution of Family Conflict*. New York: Free Press.

Johnston, J.R., L.E.G. Campbell, and S.S. Mayes (1985). Latency children in post-separation and divorce disputes. *Journal of the American Academy of Child Psychiatry*, 24(5): 563–74.

Johnston, J.R., L.E.G. Campbell, and M. Tall (1985). Impasses to the resolution of custody and visitation disputes. *American Journal of Orthopsychiatry*, 55(1): 112–29.

Johnston, J.R., R. Gonzàles, and L.E.G. Campbell (1987). Ongoing post-divorce conflict and child disturbance. *Journal of Abnormal Child Psychology*, 15(4): 493–509.

Johnston, J.R.., M. Kline, and J.M. Tschann (1989). Ongoing postdivorce conflict: Effects on children of joint custody and frequent access. *American Journal of Orthopsychiatry*, 59(4): 576–92.

Jones, D.P., and J.M. McGraw (1987). Reliable and fictitious accounts of sexual abuse to children. *Journal of Interpersonal Violence*, 2(1): 27–45.

Kelly, J.B. (1993). Current research on children's post divorce adjustment: No simple answers. *Family and Conciliation Courts Review*, 31(1): 29–49.

Kline, M., J.M. Tschann, J.R. Johnston, and J.S. Wallerstein (1989). Children's adjustment in joint and sole physical custody families. *Developmental Psychology*, 25(3): 430–8.

Kruk, E. (1993). *Divorce and Disengagement: Patterns of Fatherhood within and beyond Marriage*. Halifax: Fernwood Publishing.

– (1992). Psychological and structural factors contributing to the disengagement of noncustodial fathers after divorce. *Family and Conciliation Courts Review*, 30(1): 81–101, as cited in J.B. Kelly (1993).

Kübler-Ross, E. (1969). *On Death and Dying*. New York: Macmillan.

Kurdek, L.A. (1986). Custodial mothers' perceptions of visitation and payments of child support by noncustodial fathers in families with low and high levels   of pre-separation interparental conflict. *Journal of Applied Developmental Psychology*, 7(4): 307–23.

Kurdek, L.A., and B. Berg (1983). Correlates of children's adjustment to their parents' divorce. In L.A. Kurdek (ed.), *Children and Divorce: New Directions for Child Development* (No. 19). San Francisco, CA: Jossey-Bass.

Maccoby, E.E., and R.H. Mnookin (1992). *Dividing the Child: Social and Legal Dilemmas of Custody*. Cambridge, MA: Harvard University Press.

McDonough, H., and E. Hood (1996). Intimacy, Separation, and Conflict. Poster presentation. Toronto: Hospital for Sick Children.

McDonough, H., H. Radovanovic, L. Stein, A. Sagar, and E. Hood (1994). *'For Kids' Sake': A Treatment Program for High Conflict Separated Families*. Toronto: Clarke Institute of Psychiatry.

Miller, M.A., and R.H. Rahe (1997). Life changes scaling for the 1990s. *Journal of Psychosomatic Research*, 43(3): 279–92.

Radovanovic, H., C. Bartha, M. Magnatta, E. Hood, A. Sagar, and H. McDonough (1994). A follow-up of families disputing child custody/access: Assessment, settlement, and family relationship outcomes. *Behavioral Sciences and the Law*, 12: 427–35.

Ricci, I. (1980). *Mom's House, Dad's House: Making Two Homes for Your Child*. New York: Simon and Schuster.

Robson, B.E. (1986). The impact of divorce and separation on children. *Contemporary Pediatrics*, November/December: 6–13.

Thoennes, N., and P.G. Tjaden (1990). The extent, nature, and validity of sexual abuse allegations in custody/visitation disputes. *Child Abuse and Neglect*, 14(2): 151–63.

Trafford, A. (1982). *Crazy Time: Surviving Divorce and Building a New Life*. New York: HarperCollins.

Wakefield, H., and R. Underwager (1991). Sexual abuse allegations in divorce and custody disputes. *Behavioral Sciences and the Law*, 9: 451–68.

Wallerstein, J.S. (1985). The overburdened child: Some long-term consequences of divorce. *Social Work*, March/April: 116–23.

– (1983). Children of divorce: The psychological tasks of the child. *American Journal of Orthopsychiatry*, 53(2): 230–43.

Wallerstein, J.S., and J.B. Kelly (1980). *Surviving the Breakup: How Children and Parents Cope with Divorce*. New York: Basic Books.

– (1974). The effects of parental divorce: The adolescent experience. In E.J. Anthony and C. Koupernik (eds.), *The Child in His Family: Children Psychiatric Risk*, 3: 479–505. New York: Wiley and Sons.

Warshak, R., and J. Santrock (1983). The impact of divorce in father custody and mother custody homes: The child's perspective. In L.A. Kurdek (ed.), *Children and Divorce*. San Francisco, CA: Jossey Bass.

Winnicott, D.W. (1965). *The Maturational Processes and the Facilitating Environment. Studies in the Theory of Emotional Development*. Connecticut: International Universities Press.